YORKSHIRE DALES
TRAVEL GUIDE 2025-2026

Exploring England's Hidden Paradise – From Rolling Hills and Picturesque Villages to Secret Valleys, Historic Castles, and the Untouched Beauty of Yorkshire's Countryside

ALL RIGHTS RESERVED

No part of this publication by **DORIS S. CARVER** may be reproduced, distributed, or transmitted in any form or by any means, including photocopying, recording, or other electronic or mechanical methods, without the prior written permission of the publisher, except in the case of brief quotations embodied in critical reviews and certain other noncommercial uses permitted by copyright law.

TABLE OF CONTENT

Chapter 1: Welcome to the Yorkshire Dales — **4**
- 1.1 Discovering the Dales — 4
- 1.2 Why Visit in 2025–2026 — 8
- 1.3 Geology, Wildlife & Landscapes — 12
- 1.4 History of the National Park — 16
- 1.5 Conservation, Access & Park Authority — 20

Chapter 2: Planning Your Trip — **24**
- 2.1 When to Visit: Seasons & Weather — 24
- 2.2 Getting to the Yorkshire Dales — 26
- 2.3 Transportation Within the Park — 31
- 2.4 Entry Information & Park Access Points — 35
- 2.5 Visitor Centres & Official Support — 39

Chapter 3: Where to Stay in the Yorkshire Dales — **43**
- 3.1 Stone Cottages, Inns & Guesthouses — 43
- 3.2 Boutique Hotels & Converted Farm Lodges — 48
- 3.3 National Park Campgrounds & Glamping — 52
- 3.4 Budget Options & Independent Hostels — 56

Chapter 4: Natural Wonders & Top Attractions — **60**
- 4.1 Malham Cove, Gordale Scar & Janet's Foss — 60
- 4.2 Aysgarth Falls & the River Ure — 64
- 4.3 Ingleborough, Whernside & Pen-y-ghent — 68
- 4.4 Ribblehead Viaduct & the Settle–Carlisle Railway — 72
- 4.5 White Scar Cave & Ingleton Waterfalls Trail — 75
- 4.6 Swaledale, Wensleydale, Wharfedale & Ribblesdale — 79
- 4.7 Hardraw Force & the Pennine Hills — 83
- 4.8 Grass Wood Nature Reserve & Limestone Pavements — 86

Chapter 5: Where to Eat & Drink in the Dales — **90**
- 5.1 Traditional Yorkshire Cuisine — 90
- 5.2 Tearooms, Bakeries & Coffee Houses — 94
- 5.3 Farm Shops, Cheese Makers & Local Producers — 98
- 5.4 Organic Cafés & Wholefood Kitchens — 102

Chapter 6: Towns, Villages & Local Life — **106**
- 6.1 Hawes & the Upper Wensleydale Area — 106
- 6.2 Grassington & Wharfedale Villages — 110
- 6.3 Reeth & Swaledale Hamlets — 114
- 6.4 Settle, Malham & Southern Dales TownsHardraw Force & the Pennine Hills — 118
- 6.5 Village Walks, Markets & Craft Traditions — 123

Chapter 7: Historic Sites & Cultural Heritage — **126**
- 7.1 Bolton Abbey & the River Wharfe — 126

7.2 Jervaulx Abbey & Hidden Monastic Ruins	130
7.3 Castles, Towers & Ancient Trails	134
7.4 Museums, Heritage Centres & Storytelling	138
Chapter 8: Outdoor Activities & Exploration	**143**
8.1 Circular Walks & Short Hikes	143
8.2 Long-Distance Trails: Pennine Way & Dales Way	147
8.3 Cycling Routes & Scenic Byways	151
8.4 Caving, Climbing & Adventure Skills	155
Chapter 9: Scenic Routes & Landscape Journeys	**160**
9.1 Driving Tours & Rural Roads	160
9.2 Self-Guided Village-to-Village Walks	163
9.3 Trails with Historic & Panoramic Appeal	167
9.4 Public Rights of Way & Open Access Land	169
Chapter 10: Travel Resources & Support	**172**
10.1 Official Websites & Information Hubs	172
10.2 Travel Apps & Offline Tools	175
10.3 Emergency Services & Park Alerts	178
10.4 Weather Forecasting & Local Radio	181
10.5 Sustainable Travel Tips & Responsible Access	183

Chapter 1:
Welcome to the Yorkshire Dales

1.1 Discovering the Dales

When the Dales First Whisper Your Name

 It usually starts with something small. A photo. A story someone told. A dream of open skies and quiet places. Then one day, you're actually here—turning off the main road and rolling into a world that doesn't rush. The Yorkshire Dales don't grab you all at once. They settle into you slowly, like sunlight warming stones. The moment you arrive, it feels like the noise of everything else just slips away. There's a stillness in the air that you don't often find in the modern world, and it speaks to something deep inside you—the part that's been longing to breathe.

The landscape stretches gently in every direction. Hills roll like waves, soft and green, brushed by wind and shadow. A line of sheep trots along the edge of a narrow lane. Their hooves tap quietly on the tarmac, and the only other sound is the hush of the breeze moving through dry grass and heather. If you open your window or step outside, you might catch the smell of rain in the air, even if the sky is blue. Here, the weather is always changing, and that's part of the charm—it keeps things alive, honest, and real.

Stone Villages That Feel Like Time Forgot Them
You'll pass through villages that look like they were drawn by hand—small, neat, and made of stone the color of old memories. The cottages sit shoulder to shoulder along winding roads, their slate roofs grey and slanted, their windows small and deep-set. Smoke curls from chimneys even in summer, because evenings can still carry a chill. You'll see flower boxes bursting with color, and ivy creeping up old pub walls—though many travelers come not for the pubs, but for the peace that seems baked into the very stones.

The villages here don't perform. They just are. Some have little shops where locals bake bread each morning, or shelves lined with homemade jam. Some have nothing more than a church bell and a postbox. You might find a wooden bench with names carved into it, placed there in memory of someone who once loved this view. There's no pressure to hurry. The Dales invite you to sit, to walk, to notice.

Every Road Feels Like a Secret Worth Keeping
Driving through the Dales is unlike any other journey. The roads dip and climb without warning, turning tightly between hedgerows and past farm gates. Sometimes you'll have to stop and reverse to let a tractor through, or slow down for a flock of sheep crossing like they own the road—which they probably do. Some lanes are barely wider than your car, lined with dry-stone walls that have stood for centuries, built stone by careful stone by hands long gone.

You don't come to the Dales to get somewhere fast. You come to follow the curves of the land, to take the long way around just to see what's over the next hill. You might spot a waterfall from your window, or a lone tree standing proud in a wide, open field. The roads here aren't just about getting from place to place. They're part of the experience, part of the story.

Sheep, Swallows, and the Quiet Kind of Wild
This is sheep country. They dot every hillside like little clouds stuck to the ground, chewing calmly, always watching. Some wear splashes of bright paint on their wool to mark their farms—blue, red, green—each color a quiet code. You'll pass lambs curled beside their mothers in spring, and in summer, the fields hum with insects and birdsong. You'll hear curlews calling out over the moorlands, and swallows diving low over rivers, their wings slicing the air like whispers.

Water That Moves Like Time Itself
The rivers here don't rush unless there's rain. Most days they move slowly, curving

through the valleys like silver ribbons, smooth and steady. Step near the banks and you'll see the water's clear enough to count the stones beneath. Kids splash in it during summer, and grown-ups sit on its edge with boots off and feet dangling. You'll find small bridges arching over the streams—some so old their stones have worn smooth from centuries of feet and hooves.

And then there are the waterfalls. Tucked away like secrets, they tumble down mossy cliffs or pour from cracks in ancient rock. Some, like Aysgarth Falls or Janet's Foss, are easy to find. Others take a bit more wandering. But when you hear the water and feel the air change, you'll know you're close. Stand nearby and you'll feel it in your chest—the rhythm, the cool spray, the quiet power of something that's been moving through these hills long before you ever came.

The Air Feels Different Here—for a Reason

It smells like grass, like cold stone, like wood smoke and something faintly sweet you can't quite name. The air in the Dales carries all kinds of stories. The wind might bring the scent of sheep or fresh hay, or maybe the damp smell of moss after rain. At higher points, where the moorland stretches out like a blanket, the breeze feels wide and open, brushing your cheeks like a quiet hello.

And when it rains—and it will rain—you'll hear it gently tapping on the slate roofs, dancing down the windows. The rain doesn't spoil things here. It brings color to the fields, makes the rivers sparkle, and fills the air with that clean, cool scent that's hard to find anywhere else. Locals will tell you, "There's no bad weather, just the wrong clothes." And they're right.

This Is a Place That Changes You Slowly
You don't need an itinerary here. You need time. Time to walk through a gate and follow a stone path across a field. Time to stand at the top of a hill and see nothing but green and sky. Time to wander into a churchyard and read the names on old stones, or to sit beside a stream and let your thoughts drift like the water. It's in these small, quiet moments that the Dales do their work.

There's something deeply healing in the way this place moves—slow, gentle, patient. It doesn't demand anything from you. It just welcomes you, quietly, steadily, and without fuss. And if you let it, it'll change the way you see things. It'll remind you that beauty doesn't have to shout, that peace doesn't need to be earned, and that sometimes, the best journeys are the ones where you stop planning and start noticing.

Go On—There's So Much More Waiting Just Ahead
The Dales aren't just a place to look at. They're a place to feel. To breathe. To belong, even if just for a little while. So take your time. Wander a little. Let the hills guide you. In the chapters ahead, you'll discover quiet trails, hidden waterfalls, friendly places to sleep, and villages that feel like home. This guide was made to walk beside you, like a local friend showing you their favorite spots.

The adventure begins here. And it only gets better.

1.2 Why Visit in 2025–2026

Something about the Dales is calling more people than ever

In 2025 and 2026, the Yorkshire Dales are pulling people in like never before. You might not even know exactly why at first. You just feel it—that soft tug to go somewhere green and quiet, somewhere older than you are, where everything moves a little slower. Maybe it's the way the world has changed lately, or maybe it's just time to breathe again. Either way, the Dales are ready for you. And they've never looked more beautiful.

Spring mornings come with cool air and birdsong. Summer brings light that lasts long into the evening. In autumn, the fields turn a golden brown, and the trees rustle with copper leaves. And winter? Winter is peaceful—frost on the stone walls, smoke curling from chimneys, the kind of hush that makes you want to slow down and listen. Every season has its own kind of magic here. And in 2025 and 2026, that magic feels stronger than ever.

Old beauty, new energy: what's happening now in the Dales

What's special about this moment in the Yorkshire Dales isn't just the views or the quiet lanes. It's the way the place is alive in new ways, while still holding onto everything people have always loved. You'll find new walking paths opened up across old moorland. Tiny village shops are filling up with handmade soaps, wool scarves, oat biscuits, and fresh cheeses from local farms. Artists are moving in and opening little studios tucked behind garden gates. Farmers are inviting visitors to meet their animals. It's not loud or touristy—it's personal. It's local. It's real.

You'll notice small signs on gates that say, "Please close behind you," or "Walkers welcome." You'll hear local voices in cafés, sharing directions or just chatting over tea. This place isn't trying to change for the world. But in its own gentle way, it's opening its arms a little wider than before. You feel welcome here, not just as a visitor, but like someone returning to something they didn't even know they'd missed.

2025 brings something rare: peace and presence in a noisy world

If you've been feeling rushed, wired, or just plain tired, you're not alone. A lot of people are. That's why more travelers are skipping the busy cities and coming here. In the Dales, your shoulders drop without you even noticing. You walk on soft earth instead of pavement. You listen to streams and birds instead of horns and engines. You look at wide skies instead of screens.

Being here changes how you move. You walk slower. You look longer. You sit down more. You start noticing little things—the smell of sheep's wool on the breeze, the creak of a farm gate, the way stone walls line the land like stories written without words. These quiet things do something deep inside you. And right now, people are ready for that kind of quiet.

New paths, old places: gentle upgrades without losing the heart

Over the last couple of years, the Yorkshire Dales have been quietly improving things—adding just enough comfort for those who want it, but never too much. You'll find better signage on hiking trails, so it's easier to find your way without getting lost. Public toilets are cleaner. Local buses now connect more villages, so you don't always need a car. And in some market towns, they've restored old train stations, bringing back slow travel in the most beautiful way.

Farmers have started offering overnight stays in their old stone barns—nothing fancy, just warm beds, big breakfasts, and views that go on forever. Some pubs now serve more vegetarian meals made with local veg. National park rangers run weekend story walks for kids and grown-ups alike. These aren't tourist traps. They're just simple steps that make the Dales feel a bit easier to step into, especially if it's your first time.

A place that never shouts — but always stays with you

The thing about the Dales is they don't try to impress you right away. There are no giant signs, no flashy ads. You might even wonder, "Is this it?" on your first day. But give it time. Let the wind tousle your hair. Sit on a bench in a stone village and just listen. Walk through a green valley with nothing but birds above and sheep beside you. That's when it happens. You start to feel something shift inside you—something slow and steady, something peaceful.

People who come here often say the same thing: they didn't expect to love it this much. But now they can't stop thinking about it. It's not just the views. It's the feeling. The feeling of something real. And right now, in 2025 and 2026, that feeling is needed more than ever.

2026 promises even more reasons to stay longer and look deeper

Next year, the national park turns its attention toward storytelling. More villages are opening up walking history trails with wooden signs carved by hand. Local guides are offering "story strolls," where you learn about shepherds, weavers, and quarrymen who once worked these hills. Heritage centres are being restored with help from old photographs and family stories passed down through generations. None of this is polished. It's rough around the edges, like the land itself. But it makes you feel like you're walking through someone's memory, not just a place on a map.

More local cafés are also popping up in tiny spots you'd never expect—converted barns, church porches, even old phone boxes. They sell warm scones, pots of tea, and jam made from the berries growing just outside. It's slow, honest food. The kind you sit with. The kind that feels like home.

A gentle welcome for everyone — no matter who you are or where you're from

Whether you're coming alone, with a partner, or with your children or your grandparents, the Dales don't ask you to be anything other than yourself. You don't need fancy gear or a lot of money. All you need is the time to walk, the heart to listen, and maybe a good waterproof coat. You'll meet people who wave from tractors, who hold open gates, who give directions with a smile. No pressure. No rush.

For people who need space—for their thoughts, their worries, or just their feet—the Dales offer that in wide, open stretches. And for those looking for connection—with land, with stories, with something deeper—you'll find it in the tiniest places. A mossy wall. A foxglove in bloom. A quiet moment on a hill, where you can see for miles and miles.

If you've been waiting for the right time — this is it

2025 and 2026 are special not because the Yorkshire Dales are suddenly trendy, but because the world is ready to see them again. Or maybe, to truly see them for the first time. After everything we've all been through, there's something healing about a place that doesn't ask for anything, but gives you everything—peace, beauty, quiet, and a kind of welcome that doesn't need words.

So don't wait for someday. The Dales are here now. The hills are green. The rivers are running. The sheep are grazing. The sky is wide. And a quiet, gentle world is waiting, just beyond the next bend in the road.

Let this be the start of something beautiful. Keep reading. Keep walking. The Yorkshire Dales are ready for you.

1.3 Geology, Wildlife & Landscapes

The Ground Beneath Your Feet Whispers of Ancient Seas

Walk anywhere in the Yorkshire Dales and the land speaks — not loudly, but in soft, steady ways. It might be the crunch of loose gravel under your boots, the smooth face of a grey rock poking through the grass, or the hollow echo when you step near a cave. What lies beneath isn't just dirt or stone — it's deep history. The Dales rest on a bed of ancient limestone, formed around 340 million years ago when this whole area was the floor of a warm, shallow sea. Back then, it was teeming with corals and tiny shell creatures. And if you look closely, you can still find their fossils, like little fingerprints left behind by a world long gone.

This limestone makes the Dales look the way they do. It shapes the cliffs, gorges, caves, and hills. It's the reason the rivers twist and drop into waterfalls. It's why the stone walls look so dry and pale — they're made from the land itself. It's also what causes the strange clints and grikes — deep cracks in the pavement-like rock that you'll see on places like Malham Cove or the top of Ingleborough. These aren't man-made. They were carved by rain and time, the land breaking apart slowly, patiently, as if breathing in geologic time.

A Living Patchwork of Wild Beauty
The landscape isn't just stone and hills. It's alive. And it changes with the seasons. In spring, the meadows burst into colour. Yellow buttercups, purple orchids, and blue forget-me-nots take over fields edged by dry-stone walls. Lambs stumble over tufts of grass, calling to their mothers, while skylarks sing from somewhere high above. The air smells clean — like new leaves, damp soil, and sometimes the sweet hint of wild garlic.

By summer, the hills turn soft green and the sheep seem to have settled into lazy rhythms. Hares dart across open land, and butterflies dance over limestone grasslands warmed by sun. The rivers run clear and cold, especially in places like the River Wharfe, where they weave through wooded valleys and open banks perfect for dipping toes. Listen long enough and you'll hear water bubbling over stone, or the splash of a trout jumping in the shade.

Autumn brings gold. Beech and rowan trees turn fiery orange, their leaves falling gently onto damp footpaths. Birds call from bare hedgerows. Squirrels rush through rustling undergrowth. The days feel quieter, deeper. Mists roll low across the valleys in the morning, and the hills hold onto the light just a little longer before night falls.

In winter, the Dales pull inward. Fields are dusted with frost or snow. Stone cottages seem to lean into the wind. Sheep wear thicker coats and cluster together. You might not see as many birds or wildflowers, but there's a different kind of beauty — a stillness that wraps the land like a blanket. And when the sun shines low through bare trees, it casts shadows long and soft, like time is slowing down.

The Creatures Who Call It Home
The Dales are filled with animals, big and small, that know how to live on this land. Red squirrels still cling to bits of ancient woodland, while deer wander quietly through hidden valleys. If you're lucky, you might spot a curlew with its long curved beak, or a dipper hopping along the rocks in a fast stream, dipping its head under water to hunt. There are owls in the barns, badgers in the hedgerows, and bats flitting across the evening sky.

In the skies above, buzzards circle, watching the land for movement. Swifts and swallows fill the summer air with their swooping dances. And in spring, the sound of lapwings — their strange, watery call — floats across moorland like a ghost. Every creature seems to belong exactly where it is, shaped by the hills and seasons, just like the people who've farmed here for hundreds of years.

Where Water Shapes the World

Water is one of the quiet forces that built this land. It slips through cracks in limestone, wears down cliffs, and forms deep underground caves. Over thousands of years, it's created places that now feel sacred — waterfalls like Aysgarth and Hardraw Force, rivers like the Swale and the Ure, and secret pools hidden in deep, mossy woods.

Water in the Dales is never still for long. It runs clear and fast, sometimes over smooth rock shelves, sometimes through narrow, foaming channels. You'll hear it before you see it — the splash, the murmur, the rush. Stand beside a fall after heavy rain and feel the sound in your chest, like the land is singing from its heart.

The Walls, the Cottages, and the Human Hand

You can't talk about the Dales without talking about the stone walls. They cross the hills like lines drawn by an old hand — straight, strong, and weather-worn. They were built without cement, stone on stone, by farmers and labourers using what the land gave them. Some are hundreds of years old. They hold in sheep, mark boundaries, and shelter wildflowers and beetles in their cracks.

The villages too — like Grassington, Reeth, or Malham — feel like they grew from the ground. Their cottages are made of the same stone as the cliffs. Their windows look out onto the same hills their builders walked. You might hear the distant bleating of sheep, the gentle hum of a kettle inside, or the quiet talk of neighbours catching up outside the post office.

More Than Just Scenery: A Feeling That Stays With You
 What makes the Dales special isn't just how they look — though they are beautiful. It's how they make you feel. They slow you down. They ask you to notice. A soft breeze across a hay meadow. The silence on a high fell. The friendly nod from a passing walker. The way your body feels more grounded, more peaceful, after just a short time outside.

Even if you come for just a few days, something about the Dales stays with you. Maybe it's the stillness, or the wide-open skies, or the sense that the land has seen many lives, and still welcomes yours. It's not loud. It doesn't shout. But it speaks — in stone, in birdsong, in wind — and if you listen, it'll find a home inside you.

Just the Beginning of the Journey
 So when you look out across the fields, or run your fingers along a mossy wall, remember: you're not just looking at pretty scenery. You're touching something ancient, alive, and full of wonder. This land has stories in every stone and stream, and this is only the start.

There's much more to see. Keep reading, and let's explore it all — together.

1.4 History of the National Park

Where Time Walks Beside You: The Ancient Roots of the Dales

Long before the Yorkshire Dales became a national park, this land was already ancient — shaped by nature over millions of years, and by people for thousands. The story begins not in castles or churches, but in caves and stone tools. Humans first arrived here around 10,000 years ago, after the last Ice Age, when the glaciers melted and exposed these valleys, cliffs, and rolling fells. They were hunters, gatherers, and early settlers — following animals, gathering berries, and taking shelter in places like Victoria Cave near Settle, where archaeologists later found tools, animal bones, and even Roman-era artifacts.

These first people walked along high ridges, made paths through forests, and left behind quiet traces. Some of the oldest signs of human life are simple — charcoal from fires, sharp stones chipped into points. But even then, people were learning from the land: where to find water, how to follow herds, how to survive winter.

Stone by Stone: The Rise of Farming and Villages

Around 6,000 years ago, the Dales began to change. Farming arrived. People cleared forest patches to grow crops and raise animals. They built simple stone houses and marked their land with low walls. In time, these early farmers shaped the land in lasting ways. You can still spot the outlines of prehistoric field systems in some places — long, straight ridges in the grass that tell a story few notice at first glance.

By the Iron Age, about 2,500 years ago, the hills held small hillforts and lookout points. People lived in roundhouses made of timber and thatch, gathered around fires, and traded goods like salt, hides, and grain. The land wasn't wild, but worked and walked and loved. And as people farmed it, they also gave it meaning. High places became sacred. Springs were seen as gifts. Stones were stood up and shaped into markers of time and ceremony.

Romans and Roads: The First Big Builders

Then came the Romans — strong, organized, and determined to connect every part of Britain to their empire. They brought roads, forts, and stone structures. In places like Bainbridge (called Virosidum by the Romans), they set up a military post to guard a strategic valley. They built roads that still lie under some of the paths we walk today.

Yet even the Romans couldn't truly tame the Dales. They came, stayed for a while, and moved on. The people here kept living in small farms and villages, working the land just as they always had. But they adopted some Roman skills — better tools, pottery, maybe even a few Latin words that stuck around in old place names.

The Age of Abbeys and Sheep: Power Shifts to Monks and Wool

The medieval period — roughly from the 1100s to the 1500s — transformed the Dales in ways we can still see and feel. This was the age of monasteries. Cistercian monks, in particular, fell in love with the peaceful isolation of the Dales. They built great stone abbeys like Fountains, Bolton, and Jervaulx — quiet places where prayer, farming, and learning went hand-in-hand.

These monks also turned the Dales into one of the most important sheep-farming regions in England. Wool was like gold back then, and the monks managed vast flocks across the hills. They built granges (farm outposts), barns, and mills — many of which still stand, repurposed into homes, tea shops, or ruins covered in ivy.

Even after the abbeys were shut down by Henry VIII in the 1530s, sheep remained the heart of the Dales economy. The dry-stone walls, the simple stone barns called "laithes," and the neat pattern of fields you see today — all come from this time. They weren't made for tourists, but for survival, for trade, for life rooted in rhythm and hard work.

Farming Families and Quiet Strength: The Dales in Early Modern Times
In the centuries after the monasteries fell, the land passed into the hands of local lords and tenant farmers. Families built small homesteads, grazed cattle and sheep, and raised hardy crops like oats and barley. Life wasn't easy, but it was steady. Children worked alongside parents. Neighbours helped each other. Folk traditions grew — stories, songs, festivals, and sayings tied to the land and seasons.

Villages like Grassington, Reeth, and Muker grew slowly, often around markets or crossing points. Churches were built and rebuilt. Schools appeared in the 1700s. And stone — always stone — remained the main building material. The Dales didn't change quickly. Its strength came from holding on, not keeping up.

Mines, Mills, and Movement: The Industrial Age Comes Knocking
In the 1800s, change began to creep in. The Dales had led. Lots of it. And for a few decades, especially in Swaledale and Wharfedale, mining boomed. Men worked deep underground in cold, dark tunnels, extracting lead ore to sell across England. They built chimneys, spoil heaps, and long "hushes" — artificial gullies used to wash away topsoil. Some of these scars remain on the hillsides today.

At the same time, mills began to appear near fast-flowing rivers. Though the Dales never industrialized like Manchester or Leeds, there were wool-spinning mills, paper mills, and lime kilns. Railways arrived too, including the famous Settle–Carlisle line, opening up the area to visitors and easier transport.

But the mining faded. The mills shut. And by the early 1900s, many young people left the Dales to seek work in cities. Farms struggled. Villages shrank. The beauty of the landscape stayed — but fewer people remained to live and work on it.

A Park Born From Love, Not Luxury
In the mid-20th century, something special happened. People began to see the Dales not just as land to use — but as land to protect. After World War II, there was a movement in Britain to give people more access to the countryside. Walkers, writers, artists, and farmers spoke up. They loved the quiet valleys, the stone villages, the windswept hills — and they didn't want to see them lost.

In 1954, the Yorkshire Dales was officially declared a national park. It wasn't about turning it into a theme park or a resort. It was about respecting what was already there — and making sure everyone, no matter where they came from, could come and enjoy it. Farmers kept farming. Villagers kept living their lives. But now there were paths to follow, signs to help, and rules to keep it clean and cared for.

A Living Park: Still Changing, Still Loved

Today, the Yorkshire Dales National Park is not frozen in time. It's alive. Over 20,000 people live within its borders — real communities with schools, shops, and traditions. It's a working landscape, shaped by dry-stone wallers, conservationists, shepherds, and teachers. It welcomes millions of visitors every year, but it still offers peace, space, and deep connection.

In 2016, the park expanded, adding parts of the Westmorland Dales and stretching closer to the Lake District. It now covers over 2,100 square kilometres. And the work of protecting it continues: restoring peat bogs, supporting local farms, teaching young people about nature and heritage.

Not Just a Place — A Way of Life

The history of the Yorkshire Dales isn't written only in books. It's written in the walls, the footpaths, the field barns, the names of hills and streams. It's spoken in accents, in the rhythm of farming life, in the scent of peat smoke on a cold evening. It's a place where the past and present hold hands — not in nostalgia, but in real, living memory.

As you walk these valleys or sit by a stone bridge, remember: you're part of this story now. You're walking where Romans marched, where monks tended sheep, where miners dug deep, where children laughed through meadow grass. The Dales welcome you — not as a visitor to a museum, but as a guest in a living, breathing land.

And this is only the beginning.

1.5 Conservation, Access & Park Authority

The Yorkshire Dales is more than a stunning landscape—it's a finely balanced living ecosystem where history, nature, agriculture, and community interweave. As one of the UK's most treasured national parks, its conservation isn't just about keeping the scenery pretty—it's about stewarding the biodiversity, heritage, livelihoods, and visitor access in harmony. This work is coordinated by the Yorkshire Dales National Park Authority (YDNPA), whose mission is to protect, enhance, and encourage understanding and enjoyment of the park's special qualities.

Description:
Conservation and access in the Yorkshire Dales go hand in hand. From restoring peatlands and managing moorlands to ensuring that walkers with mobility impairments can explore the terrain, every project aims to both protect the landscape and make it accessible. The YDNPA is a key player, but they work alongside local farmers, volunteer rangers, community groups, and national conservation charities to preserve the park's integrity. Whether maintaining ancient rights of way or encouraging biodiversity in rare

habitats, conservation efforts reflect a deep respect for the past and a clear-eyed vision for the future.

Location:

The conservation work takes place across the entire park—over 2,100 square kilometres stretching through North Yorkshire, Cumbria, and Lancashire. Key areas include Swaledale's hay meadows, limestone pavements in Malhamdale, peat bogs in upper Wharfedale, ancient woodlands near Ingleborough, and traditional farmland scattered throughout villages like Hawes, Grassington, and Reeth. The headquarters of the Yorkshire Dales National Park Authority is in Bainbridge, near Hawes (YDNPA, Yoredale, Bainbridge, DL8 3EL).

Key Features:

The Yorkshire Dales' conservation priorities cover a wide spectrum:

1. Natural Habitats and Biodiversity:

- **Hay Meadows:** Iconic for their wildflowers and pollinators, traditional hay meadows have diminished by over 97% in the UK. The Dales now hold some of the few remaining species-rich examples, and active programs like the **Meadow Links** project help farmers restore these through traditional mowing schedules, reduced fertilizers, and native seed spreading.
- **Peatlands and Blanket Bogs:** The park is home to large tracts of peat bog, vital carbon sinks that help fight climate change. Restoration includes blocking drainage ditches, replanting sphagnum moss, and controlling grazing pressures.
- **Upland Woodlands:** Ancient woodlands near Muker, Hebden, and the slopes of Ingleborough are part of the park's **Dales Woodland Strategy**, which promotes regeneration of native trees and links fragmented habitats to support red squirrels, woodland birds, and diverse fungi.
- **Limestone Pavements:** These rare geological formations host unique plant species like hart's-tongue fern and mosses. Protection involves preventing illegal removal and controlling foot traffic to reduce erosion.

2. Cultural Heritage:

Dry-stone walls, stone barns (laithes), field systems, and archaeological sites are preserved through partnership grants and public education. Projects like **Every Barn Tells a Story** raise awareness about vernacular buildings and their place in Yorkshire's farming heritage.

3. Farming and Land Management:

Traditional low-intensity farming is central to both landscape and livelihood. Schemes like **Farming in Protected Landscapes (FiPL)** help farmers carry out wildlife-friendly practices—planting hedgerows, managing floodplains, and restoring dew ponds—all while maintaining viable operations.

4. Climate Action:
The **Nature Recovery Plan** and **Climate Change Adaptation Strategy** include reducing carbon emissions, supporting regenerative farming, and improving habitat connectivity to help species shift in response to warming temperatures.

5. Accessibility and Visitor Experience:
From the **Miles Without Stiles** routes for mobility-impaired visitors to inclusive visitor centers at Grassington and Hawes, access improvements ensure the park is enjoyed by people of all ages and abilities. Ranger services, signage, and responsible tourism campaigns also help maintain this balance.

Visitor Services:
The Yorkshire Dales National Park Authority operates a wide network of facilities and outreach programs:

- **Visitor Centres:** Locations in Aysgarth Falls, Hawes, Malham, and Reeth provide information, trail guides, restrooms, gift shops, and interpretation materials.
- **Volunteer Rangers and Wardens:** Over 300 volunteers support conservation work, patrol footpaths, report wildlife sightings, and engage with the public.
- **Educational Programs:** School outreach, field days, and citizen science projects (e.g., wildlife monitoring or tree planting) foster public involvement.
- **Public Rights of Way:** The park maintains over 2,600 km of footpaths, bridleways, and byways, regularly repairing stiles, bridges, and signs to keep them safe and accessible.

Price:
Entry to the park is free. Conservation programs are publicly funded, supported by grants, donations, and partner organizations. Parking at major sites (like Malham Cove or Aysgarth Falls) costs approximately $5–$8 per day. Guided walks, workshops, and educational programs range from free to $15 per participant depending on the event.

Contact Address:
Yorkshire Dales National Park Authority
Yoredale, Bainbridge, Leyburn
North Yorkshire, DL8 3EL
Phone: +44 (0)1969 652 300
Email: info@yorkshiredales.org.uk

Website:
www.yorkshiredales.org.uk

Pro tip:
If you'd like to give back during your visit, consider volunteering for a conservation day—building walls, repairing trails, or counting butterflies. The experience deepens your connection with the land and the people who care for it.

Before your trip:
Download the YDNPA's official app or maps to locate accessible trails, wildlife hotspots, and heritage sites. Some remote routes may lack phone signals, so printed maps are recommended. Also check seasonal conservation alerts—like bird nesting season in spring—when some areas may be temporarily closed.

Bring the following essentials:
Sturdy shoes (many trails cross uneven or muddy ground), layered clothing for changing weather, a reusable water bottle, binoculars for wildlife viewing, and a notebook if you're inclined to sketch, journal, or participate in citizen science.

For your safety and theirs:
Stick to marked trails, especially in protected habitats. Avoid disturbing ground-nesting birds or delicate flora. If you see damaged walls, eroded paths, or wildlife in distress, report it to a nearby ranger or via the YDNPA website.

Conclusion:
Conservation in the Yorkshire Dales isn't just a responsibility—it's a relationship. A relationship between the land and its stewards, between visitors and locals, and between tradition and innovation. The Yorkshire Dales National Park Authority serves as the beating heart of this relationship, ensuring that this cherished landscape is not only admired today but also protected and nourished for generations to come. Whether you're following the dry-stone lines of Swaledale, spotting curlews in the spring meadows, or simply breathing deeply beneath limestone cliffs, know that you're part of a living effort to honor this place.

Chapter 2: Planning Your Trip

2.1 When to Visit: Seasons & Weather

The Dales Change with the Seasons — and Each One Has Its Magic

The Yorkshire Dales don't stay the same for long. They shift and breathe with the seasons, wearing a different face each time the year turns. One month you're walking through meadows full of wildflowers and buzzing bees, and the next you're wrapped in your coat, standing in stillness while frost glitters on the stone walls. That's part of the charm here — there's no bad time to visit, only different kinds of beauty. Whether you like sunshine and long walks or quiet lanes and cozy tea rooms, there's a perfect time waiting just for you.

Spring: Lambs, Light, and Fresh Air

Spring in the Dales feels like the world waking up. The hillsides turn green again, like someone switched the color back on after months of grey. Lambs bounce around in the fields, their tiny bleats echoing through the valleys. Dry-stone walls seem to stretch out forever, and beside them, daffodils and bluebells peek through. Rain still comes, of course — this is Yorkshire — but it's gentle and soft most days, and it brings out that sweet, earthy smell in the air. Temperatures range from 8°C to 15°C (about 46°F to 59°F), so a warm jumper and waterproof coat go a long way. If you're hoping to walk without crowds and see the Dales come back to life, this is your season.

Summer: Big Skies, Wild Meadows, and Long Walks
When summer rolls in, the Dales feel endless. Wildflower meadows glow with yellows, purples, and pinks. Butterflies flit through the air, and the sun doesn't dip behind the hills until late in the evening. The rivers run clear and cool, and you might see kids (and sometimes brave adults) splashing in the shallows. This is the most popular time of year, so towns like Grassington, Hawes, and Malham get busier — especially during school holidays. But even then, you can walk just fifteen minutes out and find complete silence. Days often reach 18°C to 22°C (64°F to 72°F), though heatwaves have started pushing it higher in recent years. It's the best time for picnics, long hikes, waterfalls, and sweeping views.

Autumn: Golden Fields and Quiet Paths
Autumn might just be the Dales at their most peaceful. The air gets crisper, and the land turns gold, rust, and brown. Bracken rustles underfoot, and the wind carries the scent of wood smoke from cottage chimneys. Leaves drift down like feathers along the country lanes. Walkers still come, but fewer than in summer, so the paths feel your own. It's also the time of year when you'll spot red squirrels darting about and hear the deep calls of deer echoing through the trees. Expect temperatures between 8°C and 15°C (46°F to 59°F), and bring a good waterproof — the skies can change in minutes. If you like calm, quiet, and color, this is your moment.

Winter: Stillness, Snow, and Fireside Warmth
In winter, the Yorkshire Dales slow right down. Snow might dust the tops of Pen-y-ghent and Ingleborough, turning them white and still. Icicles hang from the barn roofs, and the lanes wind through a quiet world of grey stone and silver frost. It's not the time for long hikes — though you can still walk carefully — but it's perfect for slow days, warm cups of tea, and local stories beside a crackling fire. The towns and villages feel like postcards — lit up with fairy lights, their shops full of wool blankets, homemade pies, and friendly chatter. Temperatures can dip to 0°C (32°F) or lower, especially at night, so dress well and let the cold sharpen your senses. You won't forget the way it feels to walk in the stillness, the only sound is your boots crunching on frozen grass.

Things to Think About When Choosing Your Dates
Every season has its pros and quirks, but a few things can help you choose when to come. First, the Yorkshire Dales aren't built for big heat or heavy snow — roads can get slippery, and rural buses may stop during bad weather. If you're relying on public

transport, spring and summer are the easiest. If you're driving, remember the narrow lanes and sudden bends, especially when fog rolls in during autumn or winter. Festivals pop up throughout the year — like the Grassington Festival in June or the Yorkshire Dales Cheese Festival in September — so it's worth checking local listings. And always book your accommodation early in summer and school holidays — the best spots fill quickly.

Local Insight: How the Light Changes Everything
One thing you'll hear locals say — and it's true — is how different the Dales feel depending on the light. In summer, the long evenings paint the hills soft gold. In autumn, the low sun casts long shadows that stretch over the fields. Winter light is pale and watery, like a faded painting, while spring bursts bright and clear. These moods shape your whole day — they color the stone walls, deepen the riverbeds, and soften the sheep's wool as they graze. It's something photos can't fully capture, but your eyes — and heart — will feel it when you're here.

What to Pack for the Dales Weather
You don't need fancy gear to enjoy the Dales. Just bring good walking shoes, a waterproof coat, warm layers, and a little bag for snacks and water. If you're visiting in summer, don't forget sunscreen and a hat — even when it's cloudy, the sun still burns. In winter, gloves and thick socks are your best friends. And always carry a small torch or headlamp if you're planning to walk late — the light fades fast in the valleys.

No Matter the Month, You'll Find Beauty Here
The Dales don't try to impress with grand buildings or shiny lights. They win you over slowly, with their honesty, peace, and deep-down charm. Some folks come in summer and fall in love with the color. Others visit in winter and carry home memories of silence and soft snow. Whenever you come, the land will meet you where you are — whether you need a quiet rest, a grand adventure, or just a bit of fresh air and beauty.

So take your time. Flip through the seasons. Picture yourself walking a quiet lane, the sky wide and clear above you, the stone walls warm under your hand. Then choose the time that feels right for you — and let the Dales do the rest.

2.2 Getting to the Yorkshire Dales

The journey to somewhere slower
Getting to the Yorkshire Dales isn't about rushing. It's about starting to slow down before you even arrive. As the busy towns fade behind you and the roads narrow, it feels like the world softens too. The air changes. The hills roll out ahead like waves in green and gold. You might spot dry-stone walls stretching out in every direction, little villages tucked into the folds of the land, and sheep calmly grazing like they've always been

there. Reaching the Dales isn't just travel — it's the beginning of breathing deeper, looking closer, and letting go of hurry.

By car: follow the quiet roads that wind through time

If you want to explore freely, with the windows down and at your own pace, driving is the best way. The Yorkshire Dales National Park is spread across more than 800 square miles, and many of its loveliest corners are tucked away on quiet country lanes. From Leeds or Manchester, you can be in the Dales in about an hour and a half by car. The drive up from London takes about 4 to 5 hours, depending on traffic, but once you pass the last big motorway signs and start climbing into the hills, the views make every mile worth it.

The A65, A684, and B6255 are some of the key roads that crisscross the park, linking places like Skipton, Hawes, Ingleton, and Grassington. Some roads are narrow and winding, with stone walls close on either side — so take your time and enjoy the slow travel feel. You'll likely stop more than once just to take in a view or say hello to a curious sheep.

By train: rolling into the past with stunning views

Trains don't reach the deepest parts of the Dales, but they can get you surprisingly close — and the ride is something special. The Settle–Carlisle Railway is one of the most beautiful lines in England, with carriages that pass over stone viaducts, through tunnels, and beside waterfalls and wild moors. It's not just a journey — it's a memory being made.

You can take a direct train from Leeds to Settle, Dent, or Ribblehead, and you'll be right at the edge of the National Park. Dent Station, for example, is the highest railway station in England. From there, you can take a local taxi, plan a walk, or stay in nearby accommodations. Skipton and Ilkley, both on the edge of the Dales, are also well connected to Leeds and Bradford by rail.

By coach or bus: budget-friendly with fewer stops

If you're travelling light and want to save money, national coach lines like National Express and Megabus offer routes to nearby towns such as Skipton, Harrogate, and Richmond. From there, you'll need to switch to a local bus or taxi to reach your final stop inside the Dales.

During the summer months, the DalesBus network expands its services, especially on weekends. These buses go to popular villages and walking spots like Malham, Bolton Abbey, and Aysgarth Falls. They're a good way to travel sustainably and take in the scenery without driving, but timetables can be limited — especially in winter — so it's important to plan ahead.

By bike: for the bold and curious

Some travellers arrive by bicycle, especially those following long-distance routes like the Way of the Roses or the Yorkshire Dales Cycleway. It's challenging, with steep climbs and fast descents, but it offers a close, thrilling connection to the land. You'll feel the wind, smell the grass, and see every stone and shadow in a way cars can't match. If you're arriving by train, many stations have bike facilities, and some local shops rent bikes too.

Airports nearby: arriving from afar

If you're coming from abroad or a distant part of the UK, the closest airport is Leeds Bradford Airport, about an hour's drive from the southern edge of the Dales. Manchester Airport is larger, with more international flights, and is around 90 minutes to two hours away by car. Both airports offer car hire and rail connections.

From the airport, you can take a train to Skipton, Ilkley, or Leeds, and then head into the park by bus, taxi, or car rental. If you're staying in a remote cottage or rural B&B, contact your host ahead of time — many are happy to help arrange pickups or advise on the best route.

Local taxis: helpful but sometimes far apart

In many of the towns and larger villages, you'll find small local taxi firms. They're especially useful if you're staying somewhere quiet and need to get to a train station or walking trail. But because the distances between villages can be long, it's best to book taxis in advance. Don't expect to flag one down like in a city — call ahead, and give them plenty of notice.

Before you go: know the rhythm of the Dales

The Yorkshire Dales isn't a place of hustle and bustle. Buses don't run every hour.

Shops may close early. Taxis may be hard to reach on short notice. This quiet rhythm is part of the park's charm — but it means you should plan your travel ahead, especially in winter or midweek. Download bus timetables, check train connections, and confirm your arrival plans with your host. The more prepared you are, the more relaxed your journey will feel.

Just getting there can change the way you see the world
 By the time you reach the Yorkshire Dales, whether by train, car, bike, or bus, you'll already feel a little different. Slower. Calmer. More awake to the little things. That's part of the magic. The Dales invite you to come not just with luggage, but with open eyes. And it all begins with how you arrive.

2.3 Transportation Within the Park

Getting around slowly, deeply, and well

Once you arrive in the Yorkshire Dales, transportation becomes more than just a matter of logistics. It's about how you move through the land, how deeply you notice your surroundings, and how freely you can explore. The park is full of quiet roads, winding footpaths, ancient bridleways, and scenic drives. But unlike in cities or even larger towns, getting around here isn't always fast or frequent — and that's exactly why it's special. Whether you're walking from village to village, riding a heritage bus, or driving at a pace that lets you wave to passing hikers, moving through the Dales is part of the experience, not separate from it.

Driving: flexibility in your hands, but with care
If you want complete freedom to explore the Dales on your own schedule, having a car is the most flexible option. Roads connect nearly all of the park's small towns and villages, though they're often narrow, winding, and bordered by stone walls or grazing sheep. Some of the most scenic drives include the Buttertubs Pass between Hawes and Swaledale, the road from Malham to Arncliffe through deep limestone valleys, and the remote moorland route from Kettlewell to Coverdale.

Driving here takes patience and courtesy. Passing places are common on single-track roads — use them generously and always greet other drivers with a wave. Speed limits are generally low, and should be followed not just for safety, but to soak in the stunning views. Always watch for walkers, cyclists, sheep, and sudden weather shifts.

Parking is available in most towns and popular trailheads, usually managed by the Yorkshire Dales National Park Authority. Car parks often have pay-and-display machines, with rates around £1.50–£5 per day depending on location. Some rural sites may be cash only, so carry coins. In summer and on weekends, parking can fill quickly — arrive early or choose lesser-known spots to avoid crowds.

Walking: the best way to know the land
There is no better way to experience the Dales than on foot. This is a walking park — a place where every path reveals a new view, every stone wall tells a story, and every style leads to something quiet and extraordinary. Hundreds of miles of public rights of way crisscross the land, from short village loops to multi-day treks like the Dales Way or Pennine Way.

Many towns serve as great walking hubs: Malham, Grassington, Reeth, Hawes, and Settle all offer direct access to breathtaking routes. Even if you're not planning a long hike, you'll likely walk more than you expect — to get to waterfalls, viewpoints, or between nearby villages. Waterproof boots, an Ordnance Survey map, and a bit of curiosity are all you need to discover some of the most peaceful corners of the park.

Paths are well-marked, but rural. You may cross farmland, encounter curious livestock, or navigate uneven stone steps. Respect local rules, keep dogs on leads near animals, and close all gates behind you.

Cycling: for those who want to feel every hill
Cycling in the Dales is both rewarding and challenging. The climbs are real, the descents thrilling, and the views are always worth the effort. The Yorkshire Dales

Cycleway is a 130-mile circular route that takes in the best of the park, while smaller loop trails connect through valleys like Wharfedale, Wensleydale, and Swaledale.

Road cyclists should be prepared for steep gradients and changing weather, while off-road riders will find bridleways and gravel paths leading to quiet moors and forest edges. Bike rentals are available in towns like Settle and Hawes, and some train stations offer bike-friendly services. Always carry repair gear, a map, water, and snacks — shops can be miles apart.

DalesBus: the scenic way to explore without a car
The DalesBus network is a brilliant — if sometimes limited — way to get around the park using public transport. Run in partnership with local communities and transport groups, it offers weekend and seasonal services to some of the park's most beloved spots: Aysgarth Falls, Malham Cove, Bolton Abbey, Kettlewell, and more.

During spring, summer, and early autumn, special services like the Northern Dalesman or Wharfedale Wanderer run scenic routes with big windows and friendly drivers who often share local tips. While not designed for daily commuting, these buses are ideal for day-trippers or those who want to do a linear walk and return via a different route.

Timetables can change with the seasons, and not all routes run daily — so careful planning is essential. Updated schedules and route maps are available at www.dalesbus.org. Fares are typically under £10, with discounts for children, students, and seniors.

Local taxis: essential in a pinch, but plan ahead
In a place where buses don't always run and villages can be miles apart, local taxis can be a lifeline — especially for early morning walks, train connections, or emergency pickups. Most services are based in the larger towns: Skipton, Settle, Hawes, and Richmond. You'll need to call ahead to book, and it's best to arrange your return journey at the same time.

Because of the long distances and low population, taxis can be expensive — expect to pay £10–£25 for short journeys, and more for longer transfers. Many accommodation providers will recommend a trusted local driver or arrange transport for you.

Guided tours and walking services: travel with stories
For visitors who want to go deeper without the burden of planning, several companies offer guided walking tours, minibus explorations, and themed excursions — from geology-focused hikes to farm-to-fork food trails. These guides are often locals who know the quiet backroads, hidden ruins, and history behind the hills.

Services like Where2Walk, Muddy Boots Walking Holidays, and Dales Experience offer both day trips and multi-day journeys. Whether you're interested in ancient abbeys, waterfalls, or literary landmarks, these tours help bring the Dales to life with stories and insights you might miss on your own.

Mobility access: thoughtful, but still developing

The Yorkshire Dales National Park Authority continues to work on improving accessibility for visitors with limited mobility. Several key sites — like Malham Tarn, Grassington National Park Centre, and Aysgarth Falls — offer accessible parking, toilets, and paths. Tramper mobility scooters are available for hire at some locations, and "Miles Without Stiles" routes (gently graded paths) are growing in number.

Still, the rugged terrain and historic landscapes mean full accessibility can be a challenge. Contact the park authority or local visitor centres ahead of time to plan routes and confirm available services.

Pro tip: travel light, move slow, and ask locals

The best travel tip inside the Dales is simple: go slow. Whether by foot, car, bike, or bus, this landscape reveals itself in layers. Don't try to rush it. Instead, choose a few places and explore them deeply. Talk to locals. Ask in a café which path is blooming with heather, or which farm makes the best cheese. The people who live here often offer the kind of advice you won't find in guidebooks.

Before your trip: mix transport modes for freedom

The most rewarding way to explore the Dales is to combine travel types. Drive into the park, then leave the car and take a bus into the hills. Hike to a village, have lunch, and catch a taxi back. Bike from one market town to the next and stop overnight in a stone inn. Mixing your travel not only eases pressure on roads and parking — it opens up more meaningful moments.

Getting around the Dales isn't just movement — it's immersion

Every path, road, and bus route in the Yorkshire Dales leads somewhere beautiful. But more than that, it invites you into a different pace of life. One where you notice the sky changing over a valley. Where a lone barn on a hillside becomes your landmark. Getting lost for a moment feels like finding something. In the Dales, transportation isn't just about getting from A to B — it's about how you travel through beauty, quietly and fully present.

2.4 Entry Information & Park Access Points

Arriving into openness, not gates

Unlike many national parks around the world, the Yorkshire Dales has no main entrance, no admission fee, and no perimeter fences. It's a living, working landscape — with farms, stone-built villages, and open moorland — through which visitors are welcome to roam freely. This accessibility is one of the park's defining features: it feels more like being invited into a community than entering a managed site. Still, knowing how and where to enter the park makes all the difference in crafting a smooth and enriching visit.

No tickets, no tolls — just a landscape shared

The Yorkshire Dales National Park does not charge for entry. There are no tickets, wristbands, or turnstiles. Visitors can come and go at any time of day, year-round. You don't need a permit to hike, picnic, or photograph, and you can access almost all public rights of way and open access land freely. The only fees you may encounter relate to car parking, guided tours, or admission to specific attractions within the park such as historic houses, caves, or gardens — most of which are run independently.

Open access: your right to roam
Much of the park is designated as "open access land" under the Countryside and Rights of Way Act 2000. This means you can walk (but not camp, bike, or drive) across vast upland areas such as moorlands and fell tops, even if no footpath is marked. This is a powerful right — one that reflects the park's commitment to shared enjoyment of nature — but it comes with responsibilities. Always respect the land, avoid disturbing wildlife or livestock, and follow any temporary restriction notices (for example, during lambing season or fire-risk periods).

Most-used park access points: hubs that help you start smart
Although the entire park is open and unfenced, there are natural arrival points — towns, villages, and visitor centres — that serve as orientation hubs. These are excellent places to park, gather information, buy maps, get local advice, or start your walks.

Grassington (Wharfedale)
Located in the southern Dales and easily accessible from Skipton, Grassington is a charming town with a National Park Centre, pay-and-display car park, public toilets, cafés, and access to walks along the River Wharfe, to Linton Falls, and up to Grassington Moor. It's one of the best starting points for visitors arriving by public transport.

Malham (Malhamdale)
This popular gateway offers access to Malham Cove, Gordale Scar, Janet's Foss, and the Pennine Way. Malham has a visitor car park (£3–£5/day), public toilets, and a visitor centre with seasonal staff, maps, and displays. It's an excellent entry point for those exploring the park's famous limestone features.

Hawes (Wensleydale)
Situated in the northern Dales, Hawes is a vibrant market town offering parking, shops, cafés, and access to Hardraw Force, the Pennine Way, and the Yorkshire Dales Countryside Museum. It's also home to the Wensleydale Creamery. From Hawes, you can travel over the Buttertubs Pass or explore deeper into Upper Swaledale.

Aysgarth Falls (Wensleydale)
One of the most visited scenic spots in the park, Aysgarth Falls features a National Park Centre, car park, toilets, and easy access walking trails. It's a good point for families, and for those less inclined to long hikes.

Reeth (Swaledale)
A postcard-perfect village nestled in the northern Dales, Reeth is surrounded by

walking routes, cycling paths, and historic mining ruins. It serves as a quieter alternative to more crowded hubs and provides free parking and basic visitor services.

Settle (Ribblesdale)

Settle, on the western edge of the park, is a key arrival point by train on the scenic Settle–Carlisle Railway. It gives access to Ingleborough, caves like White Scar and Ingleborough Cave, and the Yorkshire Three Peaks Challenge. The town has multiple parking areas, good visitor infrastructure, and bus links to nearby trails.

Kirkby Lonsdale (Lune Valley)

Although just outside the official park boundary, this elegant market town offers a gateway into the western Dales and Lune Valley. It's well-served by public transport and has a strong cultural charm. Access the beautiful valley paths along the River Lune or drive eastward into Dentdale and beyond.

Entry by rail: scenic and smart

Two train lines skirt and cross into the park: the Settle–Carlisle Railway and the Leeds–Morecambe (Bentham) Line. Key park-access stations include:

- **Settle**: A direct link into central Ribblesdale and starting point for many hikes.
- **Ribblehead**: Ideal for the Yorkshire Three Peaks and exploring Ingleborough.
- **Garsdale**: Closest station to Hawes, with seasonal shuttle connections.
- **Dent**: The highest mainline station in England, and a remote but atmospheric gateway.

From these stations, local buses or pre-booked taxis can carry you deeper into the park. It's a sustainable, low-stress way to enter — and the views from the train are unforgettable.

Entry by road: key driving routes

The park is accessible by car via several A-roads, each entering through scenic valleys and villages:

- **A65** from Skipton or Ingleton: gives access to Malham, Settle, and Ribblesdale.
- **A684** from Leyburn or Sedbergh: brings you into Hawes and Wensleydale.
- **B6255**: crosses over the dramatic Buttertubs Pass into Swaledale.
- **B6160**: follows the Wharfe Valley through Grassington and Buckden.
- **A6108** from Ripon: leads to Middleham and Wensley.

Each of these roads offers scenic beauty but may be narrow, winding, and occasionally closed in winter due to snow or ice. Check the National Park website for updates if traveling in off-peak seasons.

Visitor permits: what you don't need — and what you might

As noted, the park does not require a general entry permit. However, there are a few exceptions and special considerations:

- **Fishing**: You'll need a rod license and sometimes a local permit from angling clubs.
- **Wild camping**: Generally not permitted, unless arranged with a landowner or done discretely and responsibly for one-night stays.
- **Caving or climbing**: May require permission or guidance depending on the site.
- **Drone use**: Strongly regulated. Check CAA and park rules before flying.

Accessibility to all: evolving infrastructure

The Yorkshire Dales National Park Authority is continuously working to improve access for all visitors, regardless of mobility or ability. Several visitor centres and nature trails — like the ones at Malham Tarn and Aysgarth — have wheelchair-accessible facilities. Some car parks reserve spaces near trailheads, and certain footpaths are designed with strollers or Tramper scooters in mind.

Before visiting, consult the park's official website or call the visitor centres to find tailored information, borrow mobility aids, or plan suitable walks.

Pro tip: use visitor centres as launchpads

The official Yorkshire Dales National Park Centres are more than just information kiosks. They're staffed by locals who can help you adjust your route based on weather, explain seasonal wildlife patterns, recommend less crowded sites, and show you updated maps. They're perfect starting points for travelers unfamiliar with the park's vast layout.

Main centres include:

- **Grassington National Park Centre** (BD23 5LB)
- **Malham National Park Centre** (BD23 4DA)
- **Aysgarth Falls National Park Centre** (DL8 3TH)
- **Hawes National Park Centre and Museum** (DL8 3NT)

Opening hours vary by season, generally 10:00–17:00 in peak months and reduced hours in winter.

Conclusion: the doors are always open, if you know where to step

The beauty of the Yorkshire Dales lies not just in its hills and rivers, but in how naturally it invites you in. There are no tickets to scan, no gates to pass, no queues to navigate. Yet the experience can be deeply enriched by knowing your entry points —

towns with character, centres with knowledge, and routes with soul. Whether you arrive by train, bus, boot, or bike, you're stepping not just into a park, but into a shared, living landscape — one that's been open to walkers and wanderers for centuries.

2.5 Visitor Centres & Official Support

When you step into the Yorkshire Dales, it's easy to feel like you're wandering into a different world — one where the air is fresh, the hills stretch for miles, and the quiet settles into your bones. But behind this peaceful beauty, there's a strong network of people and places working hard to help you enjoy your time here, safely and meaningfully. The visitor centres and park support services may not be the stars of your trip, but they're the steady hands that help guide your journey. Whether you're lost on a footpath, curious about a flower, or wondering where to find a clean toilet, these places quietly do the work of making your Dales experience smooth and memorable.

Warm welcomes at the heart of each valley

You'll find official visitor centres scattered around the Dales, tucked into the heart of villages, or beside bustling car parks, waiting with maps, local advice, and often a kind smile from someone who's lived here for years. These aren't just information booths — they're places where stories begin. Step inside and you might meet a retired farmer volunteering his afternoon to talk about his favorite trails, or a local woman who knows exactly where the orchids are blooming this week. They don't just give directions. They listen, they share, they make you feel like you belong here.

What you'll find inside: more than just maps

Inside each centre, the shelves are full of treasures. Local guidebooks written by folks who've walked every field. Handmade crafts and wool goods, fresh from nearby farms. Leaflets with walking routes, ideas for rainy days, and gentle reminders about how to keep your boots from trampling rare plants. Many centres also have small displays — like mini-museums — showing old tools, maps, photos, and tales from the past that help you understand the land under your feet.

And then, there are the essentials. Toilets that are actually clean. Baby-changing rooms. Places to refill your water bottle. Somewhere to sit and warm up on a cold day. It's the little things that make the biggest difference when you've been out in the wind all morning.

Main centres include:

Grassington National Park Centre: Just outside the busy little village of Grassington, this is one of the main hubs for visitors. With helpful staff, loads of walking suggestions, and a small exhibition, it's a great first stop if you're exploring Wharfedale.

Hawes National Park Centre: Found in the upper part of Wensleydale, this one shares a site with the Dales Countryside Museum. It offers deeper insights into the history and traditions of the area, alongside all the usual information and support services.

Malham National Park Centre: Close to the famous Malham Cove and Gordale Scar, this centre gets a lot of footfall. It's perfect for picking up trail guides, learning about local wildlife, and finding tips for navigating the busier paths safely and considerately.

Reeth National Park Centre: Located in lovely Swaledale, this centre provides a quieter base for those heading into the northern valleys. There's a small gift shop, maps, and thoughtful advice on how to get off the beaten track without getting lost.

Aysgarth Falls National Park Centre: Nestled near the beautiful cascading falls, this smaller centre is ideal for families and visitors who are keen to pair gentle strolls with dramatic views.

What makes them special: a human touch

What really sets these places apart is the kindness behind the counter. This is a land of storytellers and listeners. Ask a simple question — like "Which walk is good for today?" — and you might find yourself deep in a warm chat about weather, sheepdogs, lost Roman roads, and the best picnic spots. Locals here take pride in helping. They know that your good experience reflects their home, and they go the extra step without thinking twice.

Pro tip: Arrive early at busy centres like Malham or Grassington if you're visiting in the summer months. Parking fills quickly by mid-morning, especially on weekends or holidays.

Extra support beyond the centres

Outside the main centres, the Yorkshire Dales National Park Authority has made sure you're never really alone here. There are information boards at many car parks and trailheads with useful maps, safety tips, and news about weather or closures. You'll also find helpful waymarks and signs across the park, gently guiding your feet without breaking the natural flow of the land.

Online help, too — but with a local soul

For those who like to plan ahead, the National Park's website offers everything from printable walk guides to updates on trail conditions, event calendars, and downloadable maps. It's practical and easy to use, but still feels grounded in real local knowledge, not just distant admin.

If you need to ask a question before you come, there's a contact form and phone support — and chances are, the person replying is someone who's been out walking that same path just last weekend.

Community-run info points and hidden gems

Not all support in the Dales comes from official buildings. Many small villages have their own information points — often a room in a shop or a corner of a community hall — run by volunteers who love their home and want to share it. These places might not show up on a big map, but they're worth seeking out. They're where you'll learn about the village fête, the pop-up bakery happening Saturday morning, or the quiet trail behind the church that leads to a secret waterfall.

Accessible help for everyone

The visitor centres and park staff are always working to make the Dales more welcoming to all. Whether you need wheelchair access, want to borrow a Tramper mobility scooter, or simply need advice on the easiest walks for little legs or tired knees, there's someone ready to help. You don't have to climb a fell to feel the beauty of this place.

For your safety and theirs: If you're heading into wilder areas, especially in poor weather or shorter days, always check in at a visitor centre first. They can tell you about hazards, route changes, and whether the river crossings are safe. A ten-minute chat could save you hours of trouble.

Your first stop on a lifelong journey

Visiting the Yorkshire Dales is about more than just ticking off views. It's about feeling part of something older, quieter, and deeply rooted. The visitor centres are your doorway into that world. They give you the tools to explore wisely, the stories to understand what you're seeing, and the human warmth that makes you feel right at home.

If you've never stepped into one before, make this the trip you do. You'll walk out with more than just a map. You'll carry a bit of the Dales spirit with you — and you'll be better prepared to truly enjoy the wonders waiting just outside the door.

Chapter 3: Where to Stay in the Yorkshire Dales

3.1 Stone Cottages, Inns & Guesthouses

Stone cottages and family-run guesthouses are the heart of accommodation in the Yorkshire Dales. These stays offer a true sense of place—built from the same limestone that shapes the hills and walls outside, often passed down through generations of local families. Whether it's a shepherd's cottage on a remote hillside or a cozy inn nestled into the cobbled streets of a village, these lodgings invite visitors to slow down, breathe deeply, and feel the rhythm of Dale's life. There are no skyscraper hotels here, no chain-brand sameness. Instead, expect handmade quilts, steaming mugs by the fire, and windows that open to morning mist or bleating sheep.

Description:

This section introduces a curated selection of Yorkshire Dales accommodations known for their character, charm, and connection to the landscape. Each place is selected for authenticity, location, and guest experience. These are not just places to sleep—they are part of what makes the Dales unforgettable.

Location:
The stays listed here are found in key areas like Grassington, Reeth, Hawes, Malham, Austwick, and Bainbridge, offering access to the best walking trails, local markets, waterfalls, and scenic drives. Proximity to national park highlights is a major consideration in all selections.

Key Features:
Expect stone-built charm, wood-burning stoves, antique furniture, homemade cakes or scones on arrival, garden spaces, peaceful rural views, and the warm hospitality of local hosts. Many properties also provide local maps, guidebooks, and insider advice on where to walk, eat, or explore.

Visitor Services:
Wi-Fi is usually available but may be slower in remote spots. Many places include full English or vegetarian breakfast. Look for services like free parking, luggage storage, drying rooms for walkers, bicycle storage, and optional packed lunches. Some are pet-friendly, and several cater to families with child-friendly options.

The Traddock – Austwick, near Settle
Description:
This luxurious but unpretentious country house hotel blends elegance with deep local roots. Run by a family passionate about the area, the Georgian building is furnished with period antiques and artwork by Yorkshire artists. The kitchen uses locally sourced and organic ingredients, often from nearby farms. This is a quiet, restorative place ideal for walkers and food lovers alike.

Location:
Austwick, North Yorkshire, LA2 8BY. Just off the A65, 10 minutes from Settle and well placed for exploring the Three Peaks.

Price:
From $230 USD per night for a standard double, including breakfast.

Key Features:
Organic fine dining, dog-friendly rooms, eco-conscious practices, library, landscaped gardens, open fires.

Visitor Services:
Free Wi-Fi, afternoon tea, restaurant on-site, walking maps, packed lunch service, drying room, local taxi contacts.

Contact Address:
The Traddock, Austwick, North Yorkshire, LA2 8BY
Tel: +44 (0)15242 51224
Email: stay@thetraddock.co.uk

Website:
www.thetraddock.co.uk

Yorebridge House – Bainbridge
Description:
Set between two rivers in a quiet village, Yorebridge House is a boutique inn with style and history. The building was once a Victorian grammar school and now offers luxury with local flavor. Rooms come with deep soaking tubs, and some feature private outdoor hot tubs. It's ideal for couples seeking a peaceful base with easy access to Wensleydale's walking trails and waterfalls.

Location:
Bainbridge, Wensleydale, North Yorkshire, DL8 3EE. A short walk from the River Ure and a few miles from Hawes.

Price:
From $260 USD per night for a luxury room.

Key Features:
Gourmet food, hot tub suites, riverside location, adult-focused atmosphere, modern design with heritage charm.

Visitor Services:
Breakfast included, free parking, walking advice, Wi-Fi, dinner reservations, concierge services.

Contact Address:
Yorebridge House, Bainbridge, DL8 3EE
Tel: +44 (0)1969 652060
Email: info@yorebridgehouse.co.uk

Website:
www.yorebridgehouse.co.uk

Ashfield House – Grassington
Description:
In the lively village of Grassington, Ashfield House offers a quieter side street escape with period details and warm hospitality. The Georgian townhouse has high ceilings,

spacious rooms, and a walled garden. Breakfasts include locally smoked salmon, and the hosts often help guests plan routes or book experiences nearby.

Location:
3 Summers Fold, Grassington, Skipton, BD23 5AE. Just steps from shops, tea rooms, and the Dales Way footpath.

Price:
Around $160 USD per night for a double with breakfast.

Key Features:
Walled garden, quiet location, historic interiors, proximity to shops and walks.

Visitor Services:
Wi-Fi, drying room, free parking, breakfast to order, walking maps, guest lounge.

Contact Address:
Ashfield House, 3 Summers Fold, Grassington, BD23 5AE
Tel: +44 (0)1756 752584
Email: enquiries@ashfieldhouse.co.uk

Website:
www.ashfieldhousehotel.co.uk

The Blue Bell Inn – Kettlewell
Description:
This traditional village pub with rooms is popular with walkers tackling the Dales Way. It combines hearty local food, log fires, and simple yet comfortable rooms. The inn has been serving guests since the 1600s and continues to draw visitors for its rustic charm and warm welcome.

Location:
Kettlewell, Skipton, BD23 5QZ. A scenic 15-minute drive north of Grassington.

Price:
Rooms from $120 USD per night.

Key Features:
Historic pub setting, real ales (non-alcoholic options available), pet-friendly, scenic views of Upper Wharfedale.

Visitor Services:
Breakfast, dinner service, parking, local trail advice, dog-friendly rooms, drying area.

Contact Address:
The Blue Bell Inn, Kettlewell, BD23 5QZ
Tel: +44 (0)1756 760230
Email: info@bluebellkettlewell.co.uk

Website:
www.bluebellkettlewell.co.uk

Pro tip:
Book at least 2–3 months ahead for summer weekends or school holidays. Many of these properties only have a handful of rooms and fill quickly. If you're hiking, ask if hosts can arrange packed lunches or drop-offs at trailheads—many are happy to help.

Conclusion:
Choosing to stay in a stone cottage or a locally run guesthouse in the Dales isn't just about finding a roof—it's about feeling rooted in the place. These homes and inns offer you an invitation to slow down, live like a local, and experience the magic of Yorkshire life from the inside. Whether it's the smell of scones baking downstairs or the soft bleat of sheep in the morning, these small details turn a trip into a lasting memory.

3.2 Boutique Hotels & Converted Farm Lodges

Set against the backdrop of the Yorkshire Dales' sweeping valleys, ancient drystone walls, and winding rivers, boutique hotels and converted farm lodges offer a unique type of stay — one that blends the charm of historic rural life with modern comfort and mindful luxury. These accommodations are not large chain properties but intimate, character-rich spaces with deep ties to the local land and people. Whether nestled on a working sheep farm or tucked into a quiet lane of a centuries-old village, each property offers something distinct — warm hospitality, handmade décor, and personalized experiences that immerse guests in the atmosphere of the Dales. Staying here is not just a matter of convenience; it's an experience in itself — from waking to birdsong and mist on the fells, to sipping a mug of local herbal tea beside a stone hearth after a day of hiking.

The owners of these lodgings are often locals with generational roots in the area or newcomers drawn by the landscape and committed to preserving its traditions. They source materials and ingredients locally, support nearby artisans and farmers, and offer valuable knowledge about hidden trails, seasonal events, and places most guidebooks overlook. For those seeking both comfort and connection, boutique hotels and converted farm lodges in the Yorkshire Dales provide not only a restful base, but a bridge into the region's quiet rhythms and enduring culture.

Description:
Boutique hotels in the Yorkshire Dales are small, independently owned properties designed with attention to comfort, elegance, and a sense of place. Converted farm lodges, by contrast, are typically refurbished barns, stables, or byres — once used for agriculture — now reimagined into warm, luxurious accommodations that retain original architectural features. Thick stone walls, timber beams, and slate floors are preserved, while plush beds, rainfall showers, underfloor heating, and artisanal furnishings create a rich, sensory experience.

Many of these lodgings offer locally sourced meals, often with organic or farm-to-table options. Interiors balance rustic charm and contemporary styling — woolen throws, pottery from nearby craft studios, and curated books or maps all help guests feel both grounded and inspired. Ideal for solo travelers, couples, and small families, these properties are perfect for walking holidays, romantic getaways, writing retreats, or a quiet week away from city life.

Location:
Boutique hotels and converted farm lodges are primarily located in and around the Dales' scenic villages and valleys. Prime areas include Grassington in Wharfedale, Malham in the southern Dales, Austwick and Settle along the western edge, Reeth and Muker in Swaledale, and Bainbridge in Wensleydale. These locations provide easy access to major walking trails, waterfalls, nature reserves, and historic sites.

Price:
Prices range from approximately $130 to $300 USD per night, depending on the season, room type, and amenities. Converted lodges and family-run boutique hotels typically fall within $150–$220 USD per night for a standard double with breakfast. Luxury boutique inns and properties with private spa features may exceed $250 USD during high season.

Key Features:
Original architectural elements like exposed beams, flagstone floors, wood-burning stoves, and natural stone walls. Stylish yet comfortable rooms with en-suite bathrooms, luxury bedding, handmade furniture, and locally crafted decor. Many properties offer outdoor seating, private gardens, or patios with scenic views. Some include wellness features like in-room massage, yoga decks, or eco-conscious toiletries.

Visitor Services:
Most offer daily breakfast with seasonal, locally sourced produce; evening meals or

tasting menus may also be available. Additional services often include private parking, walking maps and guidebooks, laundry and drying rooms for wet gear, secure bike storage, Wi-Fi, and assistance booking local guides or experiences. Hosts are typically happy to arrange taxis, suggest lesser-known hikes, and accommodate dietary restrictions or special needs.

Contact Address:
Detailed below are some of the most renowned and highly rated boutique hotels and converted farm lodges in the Yorkshire Dales.

The Traddock Country House Hotel – Austwick
Description: Nestled in the village of Austwick, this award-winning family-run boutique hotel occupies a Georgian country house surrounded by gardens and limestone hills. The interiors feature antique furniture, elegant art, and a cozy lounge with open fireplaces. The in-house restaurant is organic-focused, sourcing from Yorkshire farms.
Location: Austwick, Settle, North Yorkshire, LA2 8BY
Price: From $180–$240 USD per night, including breakfast
Key Features: Elegant country-style rooms, organic fine dining, garden views, dog-friendly rooms, peaceful ambiance
Visitor Services: Full breakfast, room service, private parking, walking maps, special event hosting
Contact Address: The Traddock, Austwick, Nr Settle, North Yorkshire, LA2 8BY
Website: www.thetraddock.co.uk

Yorebridge House – Bainbridge
Description: A luxurious and stylish boutique hotel set in a former Victorian schoolhouse beside the River Ure. Each room is uniquely styled with global inspiration — one might include a Japanese soaking tub, another a Scandinavian hot tub. Known for its food, design, and spa-like touches.
Location: Bainbridge, Wensleydale, DL8 3EE
Price: From $220–$320 USD per night, with breakfast and optional dinner
Key Features: Private outdoor hot tubs, designer bathrooms, riverside setting, award-winning restaurant
Visitor Services: Room service, massage treatments by appointment, breakfast and dinner, concierge-style assistance
Contact Address: Yorebridge House, Bainbridge, DL8 3EE
Website: www.yorebridgehouse.co.uk

Low Mill Guesthouse – Bainbridge
Description: An 18th-century mill converted into an artsy and character-filled guesthouse. Original water wheels and millwork remain, integrated into stylish and welcoming rooms. Hosts are praised for their warmth and local insight.

Location: Bainbridge, North Yorkshire, DL8 3EF
Price: Around $180 USD per night including full breakfast
Key Features: Mill history, riverside charm, vintage and artisan décor, intimate atmosphere
Visitor Services: Hearty Yorkshire breakfast, local advice, complimentary refreshments
Contact Address: Low Mill Guesthouse, Bainbridge, DL8 3EF
Website: www.lowmillguesthouse.co.uk

The Black Bull Inn – Sedbergh

Description: A contemporary inn located in a traditional stone coaching inn. With minimalist interiors, culinary flair, and deep local ties, it's ideal for food-focused travelers. The menu blends local Dales ingredients with Asian-inspired cuisine.
Location: 44 Main Street, Sedbergh, Cumbria, LA10 5BL
Price: $170–$250 USD per night
Key Features: Modern design, acclaimed kitchen, village setting, excellent access to Howgill Fells
Visitor Services: Restaurant and bar, Wi-Fi, event hosting, dog-friendly, local walk suggestions
Contact Address: 44 Main Street, Sedbergh, LA10 5BL
Website: www.theblackbullsedbergh.co.uk

Swaledale Yurts – Keld (Converted Barn Lodges)

Description: A remote converted farm offering barn-style lodges with access to river trails and views of the wild Swaledale hills. Rustic yet cozy, these lodges are off-grid but comfortable, with a strong emphasis on sustainability and natural immersion.
Location: Near Keld, Swaledale, North Yorkshire, DL11 6DZ
Price: From $120–$150 USD per night
Key Features: Off-grid eco-lodges, simple interiors, natural swimming nearby, ideal for walkers
Visitor Services: Self-catering, shared kitchen and shower facilities, campfires, maps and orientation
Contact Address: Park Lodge, Keld, Richmond, DL11 6DZ
Website: www.swaledaleyurts.com

Main centres include: Grassington, Settle, Austwick, Malham, Bainbridge, Reeth, and Sedbergh — each offering a blend of proximity to walking paths, independent food shops, quiet cafés, and scenic routes.

These accommodations are more than just places to rest — they're invitations to pause, reflect, and absorb the calm richness of the Yorkshire Dales. Whether your stay includes a soak in a private outdoor hot tub under the stars, an early morning walk past dry-stone walls into misty moorland, or a conversation with your host about the land's history, you'll leave with something more lasting than photos: a sense of having truly belonged.

3.3 National Park Campgrounds & Glamping

The Yorkshire Dales offers some of England's most memorable outdoor stays, and for many travelers, nothing compares to sleeping under the stars in the heart of the park. Whether you're rolling out a sleeping bag by a crackling firepit or snuggling beneath a warm duvet in a luxury safari tent, camping and glamping in the Dales can be both rejuvenating and remarkably comfortable. It allows for a slower, immersive experience of the region — waking with the birds, cooking breakfast with mist rising over the fells, or lying back at night to watch the stars wheel overhead in one of the UK's designated Dark Sky Reserves.

Staying at a campground or glamping site in the National Park isn't just about affordability — though it's certainly budget-friendly — it's about deepening your connection to the land. Campers gain a special intimacy with the elements: morning dew on wild grass, the scent of sheep in nearby pastures, and the quiet hush that falls over the dales each evening. Many campsites are family-owned, rooted in traditional

Yorkshire farm life, offering both authenticity and warm hospitality. Meanwhile, glamping — with yurts, pods, shepherd huts, and bell tents — appeals to wellness travelers seeking comfort with nature immersion.

These sites often emphasize sustainability: compost toilets, solar-powered showers, and locally sourced breakfast baskets. They cater to all types of travelers — hikers, pilgrims, artists, spiritual seekers, or just those wanting to unplug and breathe. For faith-based, alcohol-free visitors, these locations offer a pure, peaceful alternative to busier, more commercial lodging — perfect for reflection, bonding, and connection with nature.

Description:
Campgrounds range from simple tent pitches in meadows to full-service sites with shower blocks, shops, and laundry. Some are on working farms, others in secluded valleys near rivers, woodlands, or hilltops. Glamping stays often feature pre-erected accommodations like yurts, pods, safari tents, or shepherd huts, many with wood burners, small kitchens, real beds, and even en-suite bathrooms.

These sites are perfect for multi-generational families, couples, or solo travelers who want a slower rhythm. Campfires, stargazing, and nature walks are common nightly activities. Several sites have a wellness angle, offering yoga, meditation spaces, foraging walks, or farm animal encounters.

Location:
Campgrounds and glamping sites are scattered throughout the Dales, often close to key walking trails and villages. Notable areas include:

Main centres include:
Malham and Gordale Scar (ideal for walkers), Grassington (for Dales Way proximity), Hawes and Aysgarth (in Wensleydale), Reeth and Muker (Swaledale), Ingleton and Clapham (for caves and waterfalls), and Littondale and Dentdale for more remote tranquility.

Price:
Basic tent pitches range from $20–$35 USD per night for two adults. Campervan pitches with electric hook-up usually range from $35–$50 USD. Glamping options like shepherd huts, pods, or yurts range from $80–$160 USD per night depending on amenities and season. Prices rise in summer (June–August) and school holidays. Many require advance booking, especially for glamping or weekends.

Key Features:
Campgrounds typically offer flat pitches, potable water, toilets and showers, dishwashing sinks, recycling, and sometimes a small shop or café. Glamping sites may include wood burners, hot tubs, firepits, private decks, and kitchenette facilities. Many

are dog-friendly and located near scenic footpaths. Some offer gear rentals (e.g., firewood, stoves, lanterns), covered dining shelters, or family play areas.

Visitor Services:
Most sites include helpful hosts who provide maps, walking advice, and local attraction tips. Many glamping stays provide breakfast baskets with farm eggs, bread, and preserves. Composting toilets and off-grid systems are common in eco-sites. Quiet hours, campfire guidelines, and recycling policies are strictly observed. Family services often include high chairs, baby baths, or fenced areas for safety. Some sites offer yoga classes, outdoor meditation decks, or community bonfire nights.

Contact Address:
Here are some notable campgrounds and glamping locations that stand out for their beauty, service, and immersive quality.

Usha Gap Campsite – Muker, Swaledale
Description: A peaceful, family-run site on a working sheep farm in one of the most scenic parts of Swaledale. It offers both basic and serviced pitches with spectacular views and walks starting directly from the gate.
Location: Usha Gap, Muker, Richmond, North Yorkshire, DL11 6DW
Price: $25–$40 USD per pitch per night
Key Features: Flat grass pitches, farm setting, walking trails, basic but clean amenities
Visitor Services: Toilets, hot showers, dishwashing sinks, recycling, free maps
Website: www.ushagap.co.uk

Wood Nook Caravan & Camping Park – Grassington
Description: Nestled in a sheltered former quarry woodland, this award-winning site near Grassington offers a mix of camping, caravan, and glamping pods, with high standards and a family-friendly feel.
Location: Skirethorns Lane, Threshfield, Skipton, BD23 5NU
Price: $30–$45 USD (camping), $90–$120 USD (pods)
Key Features: Woodland setting, children's play area, high-quality facilities
Visitor Services: Heated showers, electric hook-ups, laundrette, Wi-Fi, shop
Website: www.woodnook.net

Swaledale Yurts & Glamping – Near Keld
Description: A remote, riverside glamping site with Mongolian-style yurts and rustic barns, ideal for unplugging. Open fires, stargazing, and tranquil walks make this a soulful retreat.
Location: Park Lodge, Keld, DL11 6DZ
Price: $100–$150 USD per night (yurts or glamping barns)

Key Features: Dark skies, riverside setting, eco-conscious design
Visitor Services: Shared kitchen, compost toilets, yoga space, firewood sales
Website: www.swaledaleyurts.com

Howgill Lodge – Near Bolton Abbey
Description: A luxury glamping and camping park with stunning panoramic views, this site offers handcrafted timber pods and bell tents with upscale touches. Ideal for romantic or family stays.
Location: Barden, Skipton, BD23 6DJ
Price: $120–$160 USD per night for glamping
Key Features: Designer interiors, hot tubs, firepits, family-friendly setting
Visitor Services: Onsite shop, Wi-Fi, barbecue hire, breakfast hampers
Website: www.howgill-lodge.co.uk

Moss Carr Farm Glamping – Malhamdale
Description: Located on a quiet family farm near Malham, this glamping site features shepherd huts and bell tents surrounded by meadows and wildlife.
Location: Hanlith, near Malham, North Yorkshire, BD23 4BP
Price: $100–$130 USD per night
Key Features: Private meadow setting, off-grid tranquility
Visitor Services: Firewood, compost loo, small kitchen area, friendly hosts
Website: www.mosscarrfarm.co.uk

Conclusion:
Camping and glamping in the Yorkshire Dales allows travelers to step outside of routine and into rhythm with the land. Whether you're toasting marshmallows by moonlight or sipping morning tea with lambs grazing nearby, this kind of stay encourages mindfulness, connection, and rest. With options ranging from rustic to refined, these outdoor accommodations offer something for every traveler seeking simplicity and depth.

3.4 Budget Options & Independent Hostels

In a region known for sweeping valleys and storybook villages, it's heartening to find that the Yorkshire Dales still caters to budget-conscious travelers without sacrificing character or comfort. The area's budget stays — including independent hostels, bunk barns, and low-cost lodgings — offer affordable yet deeply authentic experiences for solo explorers, families, hiking groups, faith-based travelers, and students on retreat. These options are often nestled in converted stone chapels, farm buildings, and traditional dales cottages, making them a gateway to the landscape as much as a place to sleep.

Far from feeling generic or impersonal, the Dales' budget accommodations often reflect the values of their owners: community-mindedness, sustainability, and hospitality. Many are run by local charities or not-for-profits and draw in a loyal crowd of walkers along the Pennine Way, pilgrims on faith-based journeys, international backpackers, and even artists seeking solitude. With shared kitchens, common lounges, and firelit reading rooms, they encourage a warm, communal atmosphere. Clean, safe, and usually set amidst incredible scenery, they represent not just thrift but a slower, more intentional kind of travel.

Description:
Budget lodgings across the Dales typically include shared dormitories, private bunk rooms, and family rooms. You'll also find camping barns and independent hostels with self-catering kitchens, basic but clean showers, and secure gear storage for walkers and cyclists. While many options are simple, they're also full of character — think stone walls, exposed beams, wooden bunks, and windows that open to open sky and heather-covered hills.

These stays are ideal for those who value experience over luxury — hikers doing long-distance routes, parents introducing kids to the outdoors, or solo travelers looking for soulful connection with nature and others. Quiet hours, faith-friendly values, and a strong sense of respect for the land and its traditions define most of these accommodations.

Location:
Independent hostels and budget stays can be found throughout the Dales, particularly along long-distance trails like the Dales Way, Pennine Way, and Coast to Coast Path. Many are located in scenic villages or tucked away on rural farms, with easy access to walking routes, waterfalls, and nature reserves.

Main centres include:
Hawes, Malham, Kettlewell, Ingleton, Reeth, Dent, Aysgarth, and Grassington.

Price:
Dorm beds typically range from $25–$40 USD per night. Private rooms start at around $60 USD per night for two, with family rooms ranging from $80–$120 USD depending on season and facilities. Group discounts are often available for schools, faith groups, and nonprofits. Peak season (June–August and holiday weekends) fills quickly, so advance booking is essential.

Key Features:
Basic bunk-style sleeping arrangements, self-catering kitchens, shared washrooms, drying rooms for wet gear, maps and guidebooks, secure bike storage, and shared lounges or dining areas. Some include gardens, fire pits, or board game libraries. Many properties are housed in historic buildings and surrounded by countryside, making them restful and inspiring.

Visitor Services:
Friendly wardens or managers are typically on-site and provide trail info, weather updates, and local transport guidance. Most hostels offer packed lunches or breakfast by

request. Some have bookable meeting spaces or rooms for quiet reflection and group study. Sustainability practices (solar power, water conservation, recycling) are often emphasized. Quiet hours are enforced, and properties tend to be family-friendly, alcohol-free, and community-oriented.

Contact Address:

Kettlewell Hostel – Kettlewell, Wharfedale
 Description: A lively and welcoming independent hostel in a 100-year-old building, ideal for Dales Way walkers and family travelers. Offers cozy dorms and private rooms, hearty meals, and charming interiors with wood stoves and communal games.
 Location: Middle Lane, Kettlewell, Skipton, North Yorkshire, BD23 5QX
 Price: $30–$40 USD per dorm bed, $90–$110 USD for private rooms
 Key Features: Homely décor, home-cooked meals, garden, games, drying room
 Visitor Services: Breakfast and dinner available, walking maps, group bookings
 Website: www.thekettlewellhostel.co.uk

YHA Hawes – Hawes, Wensleydale
 Description: A refurbished Victorian schoolhouse turned into an affordable youth hostel, close to the Wensleydale Creamery and local waterfalls. Great for solo hikers and families alike.
 Location: Lancaster Terrace, Hawes, North Yorkshire, DL8 3LQ
 Price: $25–$35 USD for dorms, $85–$115 USD for private rooms
 Key Features: Hill views, bike storage, games room, café on-site
 Visitor Services: Wi-Fi, self-catering kitchen, lounge, maps, drying facilities
 Website: www.yha.org.uk/hostel/yha-hawes

Dales Bike Centre Bunkhouse – Fremington, Swaledale
 Description: Set in a quiet hamlet near Reeth, this simple but spotless bunkhouse caters to walkers and cyclists, with a popular café attached and scenic trails right outside the door.
 Location: Fremington, Richmond, North Yorkshire, DL11 6AW
 Price: $35–$45 USD per person per night
 Key Features: Bike storage, trail access, community vibe, eco-friendly design
 Visitor Services: Hot showers, self-catering kitchen, café, bike hire, guides
 Website: www.dalesbikecentre.co.uk

Grinton Lodge – Grinton, Swaledale
 Description: A grand 19th-century shooting lodge with panoramic views, run by YHA. It offers a mix of dorms, private rooms, and self-catering facilities in a peaceful hillside location.
 Location: Grinton, Richmond, North Yorkshire, DL11 6HS

Price: $28–$40 USD (dorm), $85–$120 USD (private)
Key Features: Historic building, games room, gardens, outdoor dining
Visitor Services: Café, laundry, Wi-Fi, self-catering options, maps, secure storage
Website: www.yha.org.uk/hostel/yha-grinton-lodge

Dent Bunkhouse – Dentdale
Description: Located in one of the quietest corners of the Dales, this charming stone bunkhouse is part of a local farm and offers basic, budget-friendly lodging with great walking access.
Location: Dent Village, Sedbergh, Cumbria, LA10 5QJ
Price: $30–$40 USD per night
Key Features: Rural setting, historic village nearby, good for groups
Visitor Services: Kitchen facilities, shared lounge, easy check-in, trail access
Website: www.dentbunkhouse.co.uk

Conclusion:
For travelers seeking affordability without compromise on beauty, comfort, or authenticity, the Yorkshire Dales' budget lodgings are a standout choice. These independent hostels and low-cost stays provide warm welcomes, well-kept facilities, and access to the land's most sacred and scenic spaces. Rooted in tradition but shaped by modern values of sustainability and inclusion, they offer community, stillness, and the deep satisfaction of traveling simply but well.

Chapter 4: Natural Wonders & Top Attractions

4.1 Malham Cove, Gordale Scar & Janet's Foss

Few places in England strike such a perfect harmony between raw geological drama and tranquil beauty as Malham Cove, Gordale Scar, and Janet's Foss. Tucked into the lush limestone folds of the southern Yorkshire Dales, these three closely connected sites form one of the most rewarding and iconic walks in the entire National Park. For generations, these landscapes have stirred the imaginations of poets, climbers, scientists, photographers, and families alike. They are at once places of challenge, meditation, folklore, and discovery. Visiting all three in a single day gives you a deeply immersive window into the soul of the Yorkshire Dales.

Together, they offer a dynamic visual story of how nature works over time—Malham Cove's dramatic limestone cliff tells of vanished glaciers; Gordale Scar's yawning chasm reveals the slow, persistent sculpting of water; and Janet's Foss, hidden in dappled woodland, murmurs with the soft magic of spring-fed falls and ancient myths. Yet this loop is not only for nature lovers or geology enthusiasts—it's equally compelling for solo travelers seeking quiet, families on a lively outdoor day, and cultural explorers wanting to feel the heartbeat of northern England's countryside.

Description:
Start with Malham Cove, the majestic limestone amphitheater formed by an ancient waterfall more than 12,000 years ago. The cliff stands over 80 meters (260 feet) tall, with sheer white-grey rock walls that have made it a favorite destination for climbers across the UK. At its base, the dry valley invites walkers to gaze upward and contemplate the immense forces that shaped it. Climb to the top, and you'll find a naturally occurring limestone pavement—a surreal, cracked stone surface split into clints and grikes. These deep fissures shelter ferns and wildflowers and offer one of the best panoramic views across Malhamdale.

From the top of the Cove, it's an easy and scenic walk toward Gordale Scar. This imposing gorge appears suddenly and dramatically—its tall limestone walls rising like a cathedral of stone, enclosing a powerful twin waterfall that gushes down from a cleft above. The water flow is variable, ranging from a gentle stream in summer to a thundering cascade after rain. Adventurous walkers often attempt the scramble beside the lower fall, but there is a safer alternative route looping around for those who prefer a more relaxed experience.

Then, just a short walk through magical ancient woodland leads to Janet's Foss—a small but enchanting waterfall tumbling into a clear pool. The name 'Foss' comes from the Norse word for waterfall, and local folklore holds that the pool is home to Janet (or Jennet), queen of the local fairies. The surrounding woodland is thick with wild garlic in spring, which fills the air with a rich, earthy scent, and the dappled sunlight gives the entire area an otherworldly feel. This is a beloved picnic spot and a refreshing final stop on the circular route.

Location:
All three attractions are located within walking distance of Malham village in the southern region of the Yorkshire Dales National Park. Malham is approximately 6.5 miles from Settle and about 11 miles from Skipton. The full circular route, beginning and ending in Malham, is approximately 4.5 miles and can be completed in 2.5 to 3.5 hours depending on pace and time spent at each site.

Use postcode **BD23 4DA** to find the National Park Visitor Centre and main car park.

Price:
There is no admission fee for Malham Cove, Gordale Scar, or Janet's Foss.

Parking in the Malham National Park Car Park costs approximately £3 for 2 hours or £5 per day (pay-and-display, accepts cards and coins).

Opening Hours:
Open-access countryside, available to visit year-round, 24 hours a day.

However, visiting during daylight hours is strongly advised for safety and ease of navigation.

Website:
www.yorkshiredales.org.uk/places/malhamdale

Key Features:
Malham Cove:

- Towering 80-meter-high curved limestone cliff
- Famous for its naturally formed limestone pavement
- Panoramic views from the top across the valley
- Popular spot for rock climbers and birdwatchers
- Home to peregrine falcons (April–August), with RSPB viewing points and staff on-site in summer

Gordale Scar:

- Dramatic, vertical limestone ravine with a thunderous waterfall
- Enclosed gorge walls rising steeply on both sides
- Rock scrambling route for the adventurous
- Geological marvel created by meltwater erosion and limestone collapse
- Surreal, almost cave-like acoustics and atmosphere

Janet's Foss:

- Charming waterfall in an enchanted woodland setting
- Mythical associations with a fairy queen
- Surrounded by lush moss, ferns, and wild garlic in spring
- Excellent family-friendly walk and picnic area
- Ideal for photography and quiet reflection

Visitor Services:
Malham village is a compact but well-equipped hub for visitors. The **Yorkshire Dales National Park Visitor Centre** (BD23 4DA) is your first stop for walking maps, trail conditions, wildlife updates, and knowledgeable local advice. Public toilets are available beside the visitor centre, and there is a small gear and souvenir shop as well.

For food and rest, the **Old Barn Café**, **The Buck Inn**, and **Beck Hall Tearoom** serve hot meals, teas, and light lunches—many offering local ingredients and vegetarian options. If you prefer to bring your own snacks, numerous picnic benches are placed throughout Malham and in the woods near Janet's Foss. Drinking water and basic medical supplies are available at the village shop.

Dogs are welcome but should be kept on leads, especially during lambing season (March to May) and near birds or livestock. In summer, RSPB staff are often on-site to help visitors spot peregrine falcons nesting on the Cove—bring binoculars or borrow some from the station.

Main centres include:
Malham Village – The base point for walks to all three sites, with visitor facilities, parking, cafés, accommodations, and a village shop.
Yorkshire Dales National Park Visitor Centre (Malham) – Maps, guides, expert staff, restrooms, and orientation information.

Pro tip:
For the most tranquil and memorable experience, begin your walk early in the morning or later in the evening—golden hour light transforms the stone into soft pastels and casts magical shadows across the valley. Avoid bank holidays if possible, as crowds can be heavy. Sturdy walking shoes with good grip are a must, especially if you plan to climb beside the waterfall at Gordale Scar. The path from Janet's Foss back to Malham is gravel and mostly level—ideal for slower walkers or families with children. Bring a light jacket even in summer, as the shade in the gorge can be cool.

Contact Address:
Yorkshire Dales National Park Visitor Centre
Malham, Skipton
North Yorkshire BD23 4DA
Phone: +44 (0)1729 833200
Email: info@yorkshiredales.org.uk

Conclusion:
Visiting Malham Cove, Gordale Scar, and Janet's Foss is not just a walk—it's a journey through ancient earth, myth, and raw beauty. Every corner of this 4.5-mile route feels lifted from a natural history documentary or a fairy tale, depending on your focus. From towering cliffs and roaring falls to mossy glades and limestone trails, this trio offers a complete portrait of what makes the Yorkshire Dales so unforgettable. It's no wonder this area draws repeat visitors and inspires generations of artists, geologists, and dreamers alike.

4.2 Aysgarth Falls & the River Ure

The Tranquil Majesty of Flowing Waterfalls in the Heart of Wensleydale

Aysgarth Falls, one of the Yorkshire Dales' most evocative natural wonders, is a symphony of water, rock, and woodland beauty that flows gently yet powerfully through Wensleydale. Spread across three wide limestone terraces—Upper, Middle, and Lower—the River Ure tumbles in cascading steps, framed by ancient trees and rich wildlife. This iconic stretch of river, beloved by poets, painters, and peaceful wanderers, has long been a place where the stillness of nature mingles with the rushing strength of water. The area's fame isn't new; artists like J. M. W. Turner once captured its essence on canvas, while modern cinema featured its dramatic beauty in *Robin Hood: Prince of Thieves*. Yet beyond the fame lies a profoundly personal place—an easy-to-reach yet soul-stirring pocket of the Dales where every visit offers a new perspective depending on light, weather, and season.

Aysgarth Falls is not a single spectacle but a sequence of evolving scenes. Visitors are invited to take their time—not just to look, but to listen, breathe, and walk. The experience here isn't about reaching a summit or racing to a viewpoint; it's about walking slowly beside flowing water, watching leaves swirl in quiet eddies, and witnessing how the river reshapes stone with time and patience. Families can enjoy the safe, well-marked paths; couples will find it an ideal romantic escape; and solo travelers will discover deep solitude beneath the woodland canopy. It's a destination that encourages not rushing but resting—a place for picnic blankets, sketchbooks, cameras, or simply stillness.

Description:
The falls are divided into three sections, each with its own rhythm and charm. The **Upper Falls**, closest to the main car park, is the most dramatic in terms of scale. Here, the River Ure fans out over a broad limestone bed, spilling in parallel ribbons down a layered drop. The roar is tangible after heavy rains, and in dry weather, the exposed rocks form natural ledges for birds and butterflies. This section also offers one of the best views for photography, especially around golden hour when the angled sunlight dances on the water.

A few minutes' walk downstream, the **Middle Falls** is often quieter and slightly more enclosed. This is where the river narrows a little, allowing for more turbulence, with moss-covered rocks creating a moody contrast to the clearer pools between the rapids. Benches line the path here, and the air feels cooler, particularly in summer, when thick foliage overhead creates a green tunnel. Many artists and photographers linger here the longest.

Finally, the **Lower Falls**, deeper into the woodlands, is a peaceful and often overlooked treasure. Here, the river relaxes. The falls are smaller, more reflective, and the surrounding trees create a feeling of being embraced by the landscape itself. Dragonflies hover over quiet pools, and if you're lucky, you may spot a heron standing still as stone at the river's edge.

Beyond the falls, the riverside trail continues alongside the River Ure through native woodland, managed carefully for biodiversity. Red squirrels and roe deer have been spotted in the underbrush, and birdlife is abundant, including dippers, wagtails, kingfishers, and the occasional barn owl. In spring, the scent of wild garlic fills the air, and bluebells carpet the forest floor. In autumn, golden leaves spin in the current, making this one of the best seasonal walks in the region.

Location:
Aysgarth Falls lies in **Wensleydale**, within the northern zone of the Yorkshire Dales National Park. The site is just off the **A684**, midway between the charming villages of **Aysgarth** and **Carperby**. The primary visitor car park and National Park Centre is signposted directly from the main road.
Postcode for navigation: DL8 3TH

Distance from major towns: About 13 miles east of Hawes, and 16 miles west of Northallerton.

Price:
Access to the falls and trails is completely **free**.
Parking at the National Park Centre operates via pay-and-display:

- £3.50 for up to 2 hours
- £5.50 for the full day
  Payment via card or cash.

Opening Hours:
The falls and public paths are open year-round, 24 hours a day.
The **National Park Centre** operates from **10:00 AM to 4:30 PM** daily, though hours may be shorter during winter months. Toilet and café facilities align with centre hours.

Website:
www.yorkshiredales.org.uk/places/aysgarth

Key Features:

- Three sequential waterfalls along the River Ure
- Accessible walking trails with waymarked routes suitable for most fitness levels
- Seasonal wildflowers including snowdrops, bluebells, wild garlic, and foxglove
- Historic features nearby including **St. Andrew's Church** with a 16th-century rood screen and an adjacent 14th-century bridge
- Cinematic history as a key filming site for *Robin Hood: Prince of Thieves*
- Wildlife sightings: dippers, herons, deer, kingfishers, and red squirrels
- Ideal conditions for both casual photography and nature sketching
- Accessible paths and benches at several viewing points
- Pet-friendly, with clear signage for leash use

Visitor Services:
The **Yorkshire Dales National Park Visitor Centre** offers maps, trail advice, wildlife guides, books, and local crafts. Knowledgeable staff can assist with walking plans or accommodation inquiries.
Toilets and **baby-changing facilities** are clean and accessible year-round.
The adjacent **Falls Café** serves hot drinks, soups, sandwiches, and locally made cakes, perfect for a riverside picnic or indoor respite. Gluten-free and plant-based options are available.
A short walk away, **Mill Race Tea Room** provides a heartier meal menu, ideal for

post-walk appetites.

Public seating is found throughout the trail system, and picnic tables are located near Upper and Lower Falls.

Dogs are welcome but must be kept on leads near livestock or nesting birds. Waste bins and bag dispensers are available at major entry points.

Limited mobility access is possible to the Upper Falls viewpoint and visitor facilities, with special parking bays near the main entrance.

Contact Address:
Aysgarth Falls National Park Centre
Aysgarth, Leyburn
North Yorkshire DL8 3TH
Phone: +44 (0)1969 662910
Email: info@yorkshiredales.org.uk

Pro tip:

If you want to experience Aysgarth Falls at its most atmospheric, visit in late autumn just after rain—the river runs high, mist curls above the falls in the early morning, and the surrounding trees blaze with copper and gold. For quieter visits, arrive early in the morning or late in the afternoon when day-trippers have gone and the forest begins to quiet. Bring binoculars if you're interested in birdwatching, and wear sturdy shoes—while paths are well maintained, they can be muddy and slick in wet weather.

Conclusion:

Aysgarth Falls and the River Ure represent everything that makes the Yorkshire Dales a treasured landscape: natural drama balanced by quiet intimacy, historic richness paired with simple joys, and the kind of scenery that invites both movement and stillness. Whether you're there for a peaceful walk, a photography expedition, or just to breathe in the river air under the trees, this trio of waterfalls offers a full-spectrum Dale experience—majestic yet manageable, wild yet welcoming.

4.3 Ingleborough, Whernside & Pen-y-ghent

The Iconic Three Peaks of the Dales – A Challenge, a Pilgrimage, a Panorama

Dominating the western skyline of the Yorkshire Dales National Park, the trio of Ingleborough, Whernside, and Pen-y-ghent stand as sentinels of the region's upland soul. Known collectively as the **Yorkshire Three Peaks**, these summits form an unmissable triangle of natural majesty, geological significance, and personal triumph for many walkers. They're not just mountains—they are milestones in memory, etched by every footstep, every breath of crisp air, and every glance across a sweeping moor or deep limestone gorge. Whether you conquer one peak at a time or take on all three in a single circuit, the experience here is raw, rewarding, and unforgettable.

These peaks rise from a dramatic landscape shaped by glaciers, water, and deep time. Each summit holds its own character: **Pen-y-ghent**, the smallest but most dramatically contoured; **Whernside**, the highest and most commanding in its views; and **Ingleborough**, the most beloved for its unique flat-topped silhouette and rich history. Together, they offer a physically engaging and emotionally profound encounter with

Yorkshire's untamed side. The area isn't just for seasoned hikers—families, solo travelers, and casual nature lovers can all find their way here, whether by a steady climb or a gentle valley walk near the base.

Description:

Pen-y-ghent (694 meters / 2,277 feet) is often the first peak tackled by those attempting the full Three Peaks Challenge. Its steep south face looks daunting from Horton-in-Ribblesdale, but the climb quickly becomes an enjoyable mix of grassy slopes, stone steps, and easy scrambling. From the summit, views stretch across Littondale, the Forest of Bowland, and even to the Lake District on a clear day. A circular route from Horton takes around 3 to 4 hours, perfect for a half-day adventure.

Whernside (736 meters / 2,415 feet) is the tallest of the three and provides the most expansive vistas. The most popular ascent begins near **Ribblehead Viaduct**, one of the great engineering icons of the Yorkshire Dales. The route to the summit is long but gradual, offering a wide-angle panorama over Dentdale, the Howgill Fells, and Morecambe Bay. Whernside's broad ridge feels wild and open—perfect for those seeking a sense of spacious solitude.

Ingleborough (723 meters / 2,372 feet) is the most distinctive in profile. Its broad, stepped flanks rise like an ancient fortress. Approaches vary, with classic routes from **Clapham**, **Horton-in-Ribblesdale**, or **Chapel-le-Dale**. The Clapham path is particularly memorable, leading through the stunning **Trow Gill** limestone gorge and past **Gaping Gill**, one of the largest known underground chambers in Britain. On top, the summit plateau offers stunning views over the Dales, the Pennines, and the distant Irish Sea.

For many visitors, these peaks are more than geographic features—they are personal challenges. The **Yorkshire Three Peaks Challenge** invites participants to climb all three summits within 12 hours, covering approximately 24 miles (38.6 km) and ascending 1,585 meters (5,200 feet). This is a rite of passage for many walkers, often raising funds for charity or testing personal endurance. However, you need not race. Each peak, visited separately and mindfully, offers rewards far beyond time or distance.

Location:

The Three Peaks lie in the western part of the Yorkshire Dales National Park, straddling **Ribblesdale** and **Chapel-le-Dale**.

- **Pen-y-ghent**: Best accessed from **Horton-in-Ribblesdale (BD24 0HE)**
- **Whernside**: Commonly climbed from **Ribblehead (LA6 3AS)**

- **Ingleborough**: Accessible via **Clapham (LA2 8EA)**, **Chapel-le-Dale**, or **Horton-in-Ribblesdale**
  Each village has train or bus connections, parking areas, and facilities.

Price:
Walking and access to the peaks is **free**.
Parking fees apply at key trailheads:

- Horton-in-Ribblesdale: £4 to £6 per day
- Clapham National Park car park: £5 for all-day use
- Ribblehead roadside parking: Free, but limited; be mindful of farm gates and passing zones

Opening Hours:
Open year-round, though weather conditions may restrict access during winter.
Long daylight hours from **May to September** are ideal for ascents.
National Park Centres (in Horton-in-Ribblesdale and Clapham):
10:00 AM – 4:30 PM (seasonal hours apply)

Website:
www.yorkshiredales.org.uk/things-to-do/yorkshire-three-peaks

Key Features:

- Three iconic summits with unique geological formations and character
- Diverse landscapes: limestone pavements, peat moorland, glacial valleys, and waterfalls
- **Gaping Gill** (near Ingleborough): 98-meter-deep natural cave occasionally open to public descents
- **Ribblehead Viaduct**: Historic 19th-century structure with striking arches beneath Whernside
- Wildlife includes skylarks, curlews, peregrine falcons, mountain hares, and even red deer in remote spots
- Extensive waymarked trails with stone flags to protect peat and reduce erosion
- Panoramic views over three counties on clear days
- Rich archaeological features including Iron Age remains near Ingleborough's summit
- Multiple circular walks and scenic valley routes for less strenuous outings
- Excellent stargazing conditions due to minimal light pollution

Visitor Services:
The **Yorkshire Dales National Park Authority** has invested in erosion control,

signposting, and visitor safety on all Three Peaks paths.

Toilets are available in Horton-in-Ribblesdale, Clapham, and near Ribblehead.

Cafés and shops offer local snacks and hiking supplies in all trailhead villages. Notable stops include:

- **Pen-y-ghent Café** (Horton): classic walker's hub with route maps and logbook
- **Old Sawmill Café** (Clapham): tea, sandwiches, and local products
- **Station Inn** (Ribblehead): serves non-alcoholic refreshments and hot food

Outdoor gear shops operate in **Settle** and **Ingleton**, with maps, boots, and waterproofs available.

Local taxi services can assist with point-to-point hiking.

Mobile signal varies; paper maps and OS app downloads are recommended.

Contact Address:
Yorkshire Dales National Park Centre – Horton-in-Ribblesdale
Main Street, Horton-in-Ribblesdale
Settle, North Yorkshire BD24 0HE
Phone: +44 (0)1749 862029
Email: info@yorkshiredales.org.uk

Pro tip:
If you're new to fellwalking, start with Pen-y-ghent—it's a manageable climb with dramatic scenery and good trails. For the full Three Peaks Challenge, begin early (by 6:00 AM) and walk clockwise from Horton. Spring and early autumn offer the best weather, but bring waterproofs, even on sunny days. Avoid weekends if you prefer solitude—the peaks are extremely popular. Carry enough water, a map, and be respectful of the land: stick to paths, close gates, and leave no trace.

Conclusion:
Ingleborough, Whernside, and Pen-y-ghent are far more than high points on a map—they are moments in time, physical tests, and gateways into the wild heart of Yorkshire. Whether tackled in a single day or savored one at a time, these peaks leave their mark, not just on boots and legs but on memory. They represent the spirit of the Dales: proud, rugged, timeless—and waiting for you.

4.4 Ribblehead Viaduct & the Settle–Carlisle Railway

An Icon of British Engineering Amidst Untamed Beauty

Rising from the remote moorlands of Batty Moss with dignified grace and quiet strength, the **Ribblehead Viaduct** is more than a feat of Victorian engineering—it is the enduring soul of the **Settle–Carlisle Railway**, etched against the dramatic backdrop of the Yorkshire Dales. Built in an era when human determination sought to conquer the challenges of landscape and distance, this 24-arched limestone structure does more than carry trains; it carries stories. Stories of the thousands of men who lived, worked, and died building it; of the wild upland that resisted every pick and hammer; and of the rail journeys that still glide across its spine today, offering passengers one of the most scenic rides in all of England.

Approaching the viaduct on foot or by rail feels almost like stepping into another time. It stands proudly alone amid the open moor, framed by the dark flanks of **Whernside** and the expansive sweep of **Ribblesdale**. Whether shrouded in morning mist, lit golden by sunset, or silhouetted in snow, the viaduct offers a changing theatre of light and weather that stirs the soul. And then there's the train—a daily ribbon of carriages crossing the arches, quietly stitching together the towns, stories, and skylines of northern England.

Description:
Constructed between **1870 and 1874**, the Ribblehead Viaduct was a key component of the ambitious **Settle–Carlisle Railway**, designed to connect Yorkshire with Scotland through the rugged terrain of the Pennines. Built primarily by a workforce of **navvies** (manual laborers), the project was as grueling as it was grand. Around 100 men lost their lives during construction due to harsh weather, poor living conditions, and accidents. The foundations were laid directly into peat bogs and unstable ground, requiring ingenuity and persistence.

The viaduct spans **400 meters (1,312 feet)** and stands **32 meters (104 feet)** high, with **24 graceful arches**, each spanning 14 meters. It remains one of the most photographed structures in the Dales, often captured with trains threading across its back like a toy set made real. Its sandstone piers blend beautifully into the natural tones of the moorland, while the surrounding terrain, rich with cotton grass and heather, gives the entire setting a feeling of stark poetry.

Beyond the viaduct lies the **Settle–Carlisle Railway** itself—a 73-mile line famous for its sweeping views, viaducts, tunnels, and sense of historic elegance. Operated today by **Northern Trains**, the route offers regular passenger service with stops in charming market towns like **Settle**, **Appleby**, and **Kirkby Stephen**, and culminates in the cathedral city of **Carlisle**. The journey is an immersion into the rural backbone of England, tracing river valleys, skimming over high moorland, and passing beneath windswept escarpments.

Location:
 Ribblehead Viaduct is located near **Ribblehead Station (LA6 3AS)**, between Settle and Ingleton, North Yorkshire.
 Access is available by car, foot, and train. A small car park lies adjacent to the viaduct with a footpath leading directly to the structure.
 GPS Coordinates: 54.2070° N, 2.3606° W

Price:
There is **no fee** to visit or walk near the viaduct.
Train tickets for the Settle–Carlisle Railway vary:

- **Single adult fares** from Settle to Carlisle: approx. **£18–£25**
- **Discounts** available for families, groups, and with railcards

- Children under 5 travel free

Opening Hours:
Open access all year for walking and photography.
Train services operate daily. Most scenic journeys:

- **Morning departure** from Settle (~9:00 AM)
- **Return** from Carlisle (~3:00–4:00 PM)

Website:
www.settle-carlisle.co.uk

Key Features:

- **Ribblehead Viaduct**: Monumental 19th-century engineering on open moorland
- **Settle–Carlisle Railway**: England's most scenic mainline train journey
- **Walking routes**: Ribblehead Circular (2–4 miles) includes views of Whernside and Blea Moor
- **Interpretive signage**: Near the viaduct explains the history and human stories of construction
- **Station Heritage Centre**: At Ribblehead Station, with exhibits and a small tearoom
- **Nearby trails**: Connect to **Whernside ascent**, **Force Gill waterfall**, and **Batty Moss meadows**
- **Dark Sky status**: Excellent stargazing location with minimal light pollution
- Seasonal wildlife includes curlews, lapwings, and redshank nesting nearby
- Railway tunnels and signal boxes visible from walking paths

Visitor Services:

- **Car parking**: Small lot near Ribblehead Station (free, but limited)
- **Toilets**: Available at Ribblehead Station
- **Ribblehead Station Heritage Centre & Café**: Seasonal opening hours, serving tea, coffee, light meals, and souvenirs
- **Nearby accommodations**: Guesthouses and B&Bs in **Ingleton**, **Horton-in-Ribblesdale**, and **Settle**
- **Public transport**: Trains and buses connect Ribblehead with surrounding villages. Check timetables in advance, especially in winter.
- Information boards and maps are posted at the site to assist with local walks and railway history

Contact Address:
Ribblehead Station Heritage Centre
Ribblehead, Carnforth, North Yorkshire LA6 3AS
Phone: +44 (0)1729 825888
Email: info@settle-carlisle.co.uk

Conclusion:
   The Ribblehead Viaduct and the Settle–Carlisle Railway aren't just destinations—they're living relics, where history and landscape meet in full grandeur. Whether you walk beneath the towering arches or ride high above the dales by rail, you'll find yourself woven into a story that spans centuries. It is Yorkshire at its most rugged and romantic, echoing with footsteps, whistles, wind—and wonder.

4.5 White Scar Cave & Ingleton Waterfalls Trail

A Journey Beneath and Alongside Yorkshire's Wildest Waters

For travelers who crave adventure layered with raw natural beauty, **White Scar Cave** and the **Ingleton Waterfalls Trail** offer a thrilling twin experience that combines underground marvels with cascading river scenery. Nestled at the edge of the limestone-rich **Ingleborough massif,** these two attractions represent the surface and subterranean drama of the Yorkshire Dales—one plunging deep into the Earth, the other ascending alongside a roaring river gorge.

Exploring both in a single day immerses you in two distinct geological worlds: first, a guided journey into the UK's longest show cave where cathedral-like chambers, underground rivers, and delicate calcite formations amaze at every turn; then, a self-guided hike through ancient oak woodland and thunderous waterfalls, where every bend in the trail reveals another cascade leaping down from the fells. The contrast—dark and light, hidden and open, dripping and tumbling—makes this pairing unforgettable.

Description:
White Scar Cave, discovered in 1923 by Cambridge student Christopher Long, is a natural limestone cave system stretching over **6 kilometers (3.7 miles)**, with around **1 mile** open to visitors via a safe, guided route. The tour lasts about **80 minutes** and leads through sculpted passageways and chambers, with highlights including the **Witch's Fingers**, **Devil's Tongue**, and the awe-inspiring **Battlefield Cavern**, which spans over **300 feet** in length and was only discovered in the 1970s.

You'll walk beside underground streams, witness fragile stalactites and stalagmites formed over tens of thousands of years, and learn about how water and time shaped the landscape above and below. Though illuminated, the cave retains its mystery and natural feel—no gaudy colored lights or commercial gimmicks here, just raw geology.

A short drive or 40-minute walk south takes you to the entrance of the **Ingleton Waterfalls Trail**, a **4.3-mile circular hike** that winds along two rivers: the **River Twiss** and **River Doe**. The path, well-maintained and waymarked, features **six named waterfalls**, including **Pecca Falls**, **Thornton Force**, and **Beezley Falls**—each unique in character. The most iconic, **Thornton Force**, plunges over a limestone cliff formed during the Carboniferous period and is a popular photography and picnic spot.

The trail includes woodland glades, ravine-side boardwalks, airy open fells, and scenic bridges—making it ideal for families, couples, and solo nature-lovers seeking an immersive half-day out. It's particularly stunning in spring, when wild garlic carpets the forest floor, and in autumn, when golden leaves frame the tumbling waters.

Location:

- **White Scar Cave**: Near Ingleton, Carnforth, North Yorkshire, LA6 3AW
  Located on the B6255 road to Hawes, just outside the village of Ingleton
- **Ingleton Waterfalls Trail**: Main entrance at Broadwood Entrance Car Park, Ingleton, LA6 3ET
  Both sites are approx. 2 miles apart; reachable by foot, car, or bicycle

Price:

- **White Scar Cave:**
  Adults: £14.00
  Children (under 15): £7.00
  Family ticket (2 adults + 2 children): £37.00
  Group discounts available; under-3s not permitted in cave
- **Ingleton Waterfalls Trail:**
  Adults: £10.00
  Children (under 16): £5.00
  Under 3s: Free
  Price includes access to maintained trail, bridges, and rest facilities

Opening Hours:

- **White Scar Cave:**
  Open daily from mid-February to late November
  First tour at 10:20 AM; last tour around 4:00 PM (varies by season)
  Winter: closed or limited access (check website for winter opening)
- **Ingleton Waterfalls Trail:**
  Open year-round, dawn to dusk
  Entry gate manned from 9:00 AM to 4:00 PM (ticket office hours)
  Trail typically takes 2.5–4 hours to complete

Website:

- White Scar Cave: www.whitescarcave.co.uk
- Ingleton Waterfalls Trail: www.ingletonwaterfallstrail.co.uk

Key Features:

- **White Scar Cave:**
  - UK's longest show cave open to the public
  - Spectacular natural formations: stalactites, flowstone, underground waterfalls
  - Battlefield Cavern: one of Britain's largest natural cave chambers
  - Guided tour with expert narration
  - Visitor centre and riverside picnic area with views of Ingleborough
- **Ingleton Waterfalls Trail:**
  - Six named waterfalls including Thornton Force and Pecca Twin Falls
  - Dramatic limestone gorge landscapes and tranquil forest paths
  - Interpretive signs explaining geology, flora, and wildlife

- Panoramic views over the Dales from high points
- Well-maintained paths and bridges; sturdy footwear recommended

Visitor Services:

- **White Scar Cave**:
    - Free car park and picnic area
    - Café (open seasonally) serving light snacks, coffee, and tea
    - Toilets available at visitor centre
    - Gift shop with minerals, books, and local crafts
    - Waterproof jackets recommended (cave is damp, 8°C year-round)
- **Ingleton Waterfalls Trail**:
    - Broadwood car park (pay-and-display) with ticket booth and map boards
    - Refreshments and café at the trail entrance (open daily in summer)
    - Toilets at entrance and mid-trail rest area
    - Benches, picnic areas, and photo stops throughout
    - Dogs allowed but must be on leads
    - Trail closes during severe weather for safety—check ahead in winter

Contact Address:

- **White Scar Cave**
  White Scar Cave, Ingleton, Carnforth, North Yorkshire LA6 3AW
  Phone: +44 (0)15242 41244
  Email: info@whitescarcave.co.uk

- **Ingleton Waterfalls Trail**
  Broadwood Entrance, Ingleton, North Yorkshire LA6 3ET
  Phone: +44 (0)15242 41930
  Email: info@ingletonwaterfallstrail.co.uk

Pro tip:
Start with **White Scar Cave** in the morning—when it's quieter and easier to hear the guide—and then refuel with a picnic or café lunch before tackling the waterfall trail in the afternoon. Bring a waterproof layer and walking shoes with good grip for both sites. If you're staying overnight, time your visit in spring or autumn for stunning foliage and fewer crowds. Early morning and late afternoon are best for photography when the light is soft.

Conclusion:
White Scar Cave and the Ingleton Waterfalls Trail create an immersive day of discovery that reveals the full force and finesse of Yorkshire's natural landscapes. From echoing

underground caverns to sunlit falls tumbling over ancient rock, each step—above or below ground—connects you with the forces that shaped this wild and enduring corner of England. It's an experience that's equal parts thrilling, calming, and unforgettable.

4.6 Swaledale, Wensleydale, Wharfedale & Ribblesdale

The Four Great Dales: A Living Tapestry of Nature, Heritage, and Peaceful Beauty

The Yorkshire Dales derive their very name from the valleys—*dales*—that carve through the region, each one a distinct corridor of character, history, and landscape. Among the most cherished and visited are **Swaledale**, **Wensleydale**, **Wharfedale**, and **Ribblesdale**. Exploring these four dales is like wandering through a storybook of northern England—where dry-stone walls run like stitches across green patchwork hills, sheep graze undisturbed beneath wide skies, and every stone cottage, hidden waterfall, and craggy ridge tells of lives lived in quiet harmony with nature.

Each dale has its own personality and flavor. From the wild and remote upper reaches of **Swaledale**, to the chocolate-box villages and creamy cheese heritage of **Wensleydale**; from the flower-strewn meadows and artist-loved light of **Wharfedale**, to the dramatic limestone cliffs and iconic Three Peaks of **Ribblesdale**—there's an immersive richness that makes these valleys a lifetime memory. Whether you choose to cycle, hike, or simply drive slowly between scenic stops, this region offers some of the finest rural experiences in England.

Description:

   Swaledale, in the northern reaches of the Dales, is a place of stone barns, wildflower-rich hay meadows, heather moorlands, and tight, winding lanes that feel untouched by time. Its heart beats through villages like **Reeth**, **Muker**, and **Keld**, where hardy farming culture meets ancient lead mining history. The river **Swale** carves its way through dramatic scenery, with waterfalls like **Kisdon Force** hidden within wooded gorges, and sweeping views from passes like **Buttertubs**.

Just south lies **Wensleydale**, the most fertile and expansive of the dales, famous for its namesake cheese and its rolling green fields. The market town of **Hawes** is a hub for walkers and food lovers, with the **Wensleydale Creamery** offering tastings, tours, and heritage displays. Waterfalls like **Aysgarth Falls** and **Hardraw Force** lend drama, while the historic ruins of **Bolton Castle** and **Jervaulx Abbey** connect the land with medieval lore. Despite its popularity, Wensleydale remains deeply tranquil, especially in the softer light of early morning or twilight.

Further southeast is **Wharfedale**, a gentle and painterly landscape that inspired poets, painters, and early conservationists. The towns of **Grassington**, **Kettlewell**, and **Buckden** exude charm with limestone buildings, village greens, and traditional tearooms. The river **Wharfe** threads through it all, with trails like the **Dales Way** and scenic spots such as **Linton Falls** and the **Strid** near Bolton Abbey. Spring and early summer transform its meadows into brilliant tapestries of wildflowers.

Finally, **Ribblesdale**, known for its dramatic limestone features, anchors the western Dales with bold landscapes and bold adventures. This is where the famous **Three Peaks—Pen-y-ghent**, **Whernside**, and **Ingleborough**—rise steeply from the valley, challenging walkers and offering astonishing views. The **Ribblehead Viaduct**, part of the **Settle–Carlisle Railway**, is an architectural marvel set against the raw hills, while caves and potholes like **Gaping Gill** hint at the forces beneath the earth.

Location:

- **Swaledale**: Stretching west of **Richmond** through **Reeth**, **Muker**, and **Keld**, accessible via the B6270
- **Wensleydale**: From **Leyburn** to **Hawes**, following the A684 and River Ure
- **Wharfedale**: Running from **Ilkley** to **Buckden**, accessed via the B6160 and B6265
- **Ribblesdale**: From **Settle** through **Horton-in-Ribblesdale** to **Ribblehead**, along the B6479

Price:

Access to the dales and roads is free, but individual attractions, parking areas, and events may charge fees:

- **Parking**: Public car parks typically charge £1–£5 for 2–4 hours
- **Attractions**:
    - **Wensleydale Creamery Visitor Centre**: Adults £5, Children £3
    - **Bolton Castle**: Adults £12, Children £9
    - **Jervaulx Abbey (honesty box)**: Suggested donation £3
    - **Settle–Carlisle Train**: Day return tickets from Settle to Ribblehead around £8–£10

Opening Hours:

The landscapes are open year-round, dawn to dusk. Attractions and visitor centers have varying schedules:

- **Wensleydale Creamery**: 10:00 AM – 4:00 PM daily
- **Bolton Castle**: Open March–October, 10:00 AM – 5:00 PM
- **Settle–Carlisle Railway**: Trains run daily; check www.settle-carlisle.co.uk for schedules
- **National Park Centres** (in Hawes, Malham, Aysgarth): 9:30 AM – 4:30 PM

Website:

- Yorkshire Dales National Park: www.yorkshiredales.org.uk
- Wensleydale Creamery: www.wensleydale.co.uk
- Settle–Carlisle Railway: www.settle-carlisle.co.uk

Key Features:

- Distinct cultural and natural identity in each dale
- Traditional stone villages, dry-stone walls, and isolated farmsteads
- Iconic landmarks: Ribblehead Viaduct, Aysgarth Falls, Pen-y-ghent
- Cheese-making heritage and traditional crafts
- Outstanding walking and cycling routes
- Historic sites including castles, abbeys, and packhorse bridges
- Spring and autumn offer especially vivid beauty

Visitor Services:

- Multiple **National Park Information Centres** (Hawes, Aysgarth, Malham) provide maps, guides, and local tips

- Cafés, tearooms, and pubs (serving alcohol-free options and local food) in most villages
- Local bus services connect key dales and towns
- Walking route markers and rest benches along popular trails
- Public toilets at visitor centres, car parks, and main villages
- Accommodations ranging from **eco-lodges and bunk barns to guesthouses** (see Chapter 3 for details)
- Farm shops and artisan markets in **Reeth, Leyburn**, and **Grassington**

Contact Address:

- **Yorkshire Dales National Park Authority**
  Yoredale, Bainbridge, Leyburn, North Yorkshire, DL8 3EL
  Phone: +44 (0)1969 652349
  Email: info@yorkshiredales.org.uk

Pro tip:
If time is limited, choose two contrasting dales to explore—**Swaledale** for wild solitude and **Wharfedale** for lush gentleness. Visit in **late June or early July** for meadows at their peak bloom. Download the **Yorkshire Dales app** or grab printed trail maps from any visitor centre. Plan driving loops that combine scenic stops, gentle walks, and picnic viewpoints for a rich day without rushing.

Conclusion:
Swaledale, Wensleydale, Wharfedale, and Ribblesdale are more than valleys; they are soulful, living landscapes that breathe tradition and beauty into every footstep. Whether you're crossing a lonely fell, sharing scones in a stone café, or sitting beside a waterfall listening to sheep bells echoing through the hills, these four dales offer not just scenery but a deeper sense of timelessness. They invite you to slow down, look closely, and truly feel the rhythm of rural England.

4.7 Hardraw Force & the Pennine Hills

Where Waterfalls Whisper and Hills Beckon the Spirit

Tucked into the northern folds of the Yorkshire Dales, **Hardraw Force** is a hidden gem that pulses with elemental energy. Falling dramatically in a single unbroken drop of around 100 feet, it is England's tallest above-ground single-drop waterfall. But the true magic of Hardraw Force is not just its height—it's the setting: a cool, shaded glen draped in moss, surrounded by ancient woodland and birdsong, with the sound of the fall echoing softly through the gorge. Just above it, the **Pennine Hills** stretch across the horizon—rugged, silent sentinels often called the "backbone of England." This area forms one of the most stirring meeting points of geology, water, and wilderness in the entire park.

Whether you're seeking a short, soul-lifting stroll or a full day of moorland hiking, this corner of the Dales rewards all levels of walkers with raw beauty and poetic peace. The juxtaposition of the crashing waterfall below and the expansive hills above forms a layered experience—earth, water, sky—all connected in one unbroken breath of the land.

Description:
 Hardraw Force is located just outside the village of **Hawes** and is accessed via a private path that begins behind the **Green Dragon Inn**. The approach is modest—through an old courtyard and into a wooded ravine—but it quickly unfolds into a magical world. The waterfall drops in a single, clean curtain from a limestone cliff into a shallow plunge pool. The gorge was formed by glacial meltwaters, and its cool microclimate supports mosses, ferns, and birds rarely found elsewhere. Visit after rain and you'll witness the force at its most theatrical; in summer, the water flow is gentler, creating a peaceful ambiance that encourages stillness and reflection.

Beyond the fall lies the **Pennine Hills**, a line of heather-covered uplands and gritstone ridges that form the western spine of Yorkshire. These hills—particularly **Great Shunner Fell**, **Lovely Seat**, and the route over **Buttertubs Pass**—offer breathtaking views, isolated trails, and a satisfying sense of elevation above the dales. The **Pennine Way**, one of Britain's most iconic long-distance walking routes, runs right through this area. From Hardraw or Hawes, you can ascend into the Pennines for a half-day hike or continue southward over the moors toward **Tan Hill** or **Malham**. Expect big skies, curlews calling, and a tangible sense of ancient land under your boots.

Location:

- **Hardraw Force**: Just north of **Hawes**, North Yorkshire, DL8 3LZ. Entry via the **Green Dragon Inn** on Hardraw Road.
- **Pennine Hills Access Points**: From **Hawes**, **Hardraw**, or nearby **Thwaite** and **Tan Hill**, accessible via the A684 and B6270 roads.

Price:

- **Hardraw Force Entry Fee**: Adults £4, Children £2.50 (Access through Green Dragon Inn's rear gate)
- **Pennine Hills**: Free access via public footpaths and open access land
- **Parking**: Available in Hawes and Hardraw village—typically £1–£4 for a few hours

Opening Hours:

- **Hardraw Force**: Open daily, typically 10:00 AM – 5:00 PM (check seasonal hours)

- **Pennine Trails**: Open year-round, best visited during daylight hours between 8:00 AM and 7:00 PM during spring/summer
- **Visitor Centres** (e.g., Hawes): 9:30 AM – 4:30 PM

Website:

- Hardraw Force: www.hardrawforce.com
- Yorkshire Dales NP: www.yorkshiredales.org.uk
- Pennine Way info: www.nationaltrail.co.uk/en_GB/trails/pennine-way

Key Features:

- **England's tallest above-ground single-drop waterfall**
- Hidden gorge setting with moss-covered cliffs and woodland habitat
- Nearby access to the **Pennine Way** and upland hiking routes
- Photography and sketching haven in all seasons
- Picnic area near entrance; benches along paths
- Short loop trails or extended high-level walking into **Great Shunner Fell**
- Ideal for quiet spiritual walks or rugged adventure treks

Visitor Services:

- **Green Dragon Inn** offers toilets and a café with non-alcoholic refreshments
- **Public toilets** and **National Park Information Centre** in **Hawes**
- Shops, food stores, and outdoor gear rentals available in **Hawes village**
- Public bus service to **Hawes** via Richmond and Leyburn
- National Park Rangers sometimes offer guided hikes in summer
- Paths are well-marked but can be slippery near the waterfall—sturdy boots advised
- Benches and scenic spots for quiet contemplation or sketching

Contact Address:

- **Hardraw Force Visitor Entrance (via Green Dragon Inn)**
  Hardraw, Hawes, North Yorkshire, DL8 3LZ
  Phone: +44 (0)1969 667392
- **Yorkshire Dales National Park Centre (Hawes)**
  Dales Countryside Museum, Station Yard, Hawes DL8 3NT
  Phone: +44 (0)1969 666210
  Email: hawes@yorkshiredales.org.uk

Conclusion:
Hardraw Force and the Pennine Hills are more than scenic stops—they're a union of

force and stillness, of falling water and rising land. The quiet thunder of the falls, the haunting moors above, and the soft beauty of the trails below create a pocket of Yorkshire that nourishes both the adventurous and the contemplative soul. It's a place to breathe deeply, walk slowly, and let the land speak its ancient language.

4.8 Grass Wood Nature Reserve & Limestone Pavements

Where Ancient Forest Meets a Fossilized Ocean Floor

High above the meandering River Wharfe and just northwest of the village of Grassington, **Grass Wood Nature Reserve** unfolds like a living museum of natural history, time, and resilience. This is not just a walk in the woods—it's an immersion into one of the Yorkshire Dales' last remaining ancient woodlands, set atop dramatic **limestone pavements** carved by glaciers and cracked into clints and grikes that shelter rare alpine plants. These unique pavements, exposed remnants of a prehistoric seabed, now support a fragile but vibrant ecosystem unlike anywhere else in Britain.

Grass Wood's beauty lies in its contrasts: light filtering through twisted hazel and ash trees, sudden openings onto sun-bleached rock platforms, and the near-silent presence of roe deer, redstarts, and occasionally peregrine falcons overhead. Visitors come not only for the scenery, but also to experience one of the Dales' most ecologically rich and spiritually tranquil spots. It's a hidden Eden—seldom crowded, lovingly protected, and alive with natural wonder.

Description:

Covering over 80 hectares, Grass Wood is designated as a Site of Special Scientific Interest (SSSI) and a Local Nature Reserve. Unlike commercial forestry or open grazing land, this is a true semi-natural ancient woodland—meaning parts of it have been continuously wooded since at least 1600 AD. The forest includes a blend of ash, oak, hazel, birch, and wych elm, underpinned by a carpet of bluebells in spring and an ever-changing tapestry of woodland flowers. The reserve also protects multiple **limestone pavement** outcrops—flat, rocky platforms left behind after glaciers scraped off the surface soil at the end of the last Ice Age. These pavements are home to rare ferns, mosses, and arctic-alpine species nestled in their shaded crevices.

The network of trails through Grass Wood allows for peaceful, moderate hikes lasting 1 to 2 hours, with several scenic loops and access points. Paths are narrow, unpaved, and can be slippery in wet weather, so walking boots are recommended. There are no fences, lighting, or commercial facilities—just the sounds of woodland life and wind across stone.

Location:

- **Grass Wood Nature Reserve**, Grassington, North Yorkshire, BD23 5LB
- Located off Grass Wood Lane, approximately 1 mile northwest of Grassington village
- Closest town: **Grassington**, served by local buses from Skipton

Price:

- **Entry**: Free
- **Parking**: Limited free layby parking available on Grass Wood Lane; for longer stays, use paid parking in Grassington village (typically £3–£5 per day)

Opening Hours:

- Open daily, year-round
- Best visited between **8:00 AM and 6:00 PM** in spring and summer for light and bird activity
- Woodland access not recommended in strong winds due to falling branch risk

Website:

- www.ydmt.org/grass-wood
- www.ywt.org.uk – Yorkshire Wildlife Trust (for nearby limestone habitats)

Key Features:

- One of the last surviving ancient broadleaf woodlands in the Dales
- Outstanding examples of **limestone pavement** geology
- Rare arctic-alpine plants, mosses, and lichens
- Rich birdlife including wood warblers, treecreepers, and tawny owls
- Spring carpets of bluebells and early purple orchids
- Several informal trail loops, including routes to nearby **Conistone Dib** and **Scot Gate Ash**

Visitor Services:

- **No facilities on site**—no toilets, visitor centre, or cafés
- Nearest amenities (toilets, cafés, pubs, shops) are in **Grassington village**
- **Grassington National Park Centre** offers maps, guides, and local advice
- Well-marked footpaths but no paved surfaces—bring a printed map or GPS
- **Dog-friendly**, but dogs must be kept on leads to protect nesting birds
- Interpretation panels with ecological and geological facts at some entrances
- Wildlife photography, birdwatching, and botany are popular here—bring binoculars

Contact Address:

- **Grass Wood Nature Reserve**
  Grass Wood Lane, near Grassington, North Yorkshire, BD23 5LB
- **Yorkshire Dales Millennium Trust**
  Town Head Lane, Clapham, LA2 8DP
  Phone: +44 (0)15242 51002
  Email: info@ydmt.org
- **Grassington National Park Centre**
  Hebden Road, Grassington, BD23 5LB
  Phone: +44 (0)1756 751690

Pro tip:
Arrive early in late April or May to experience the woodland floor cloaked in bluebells and wild garlic. For a longer adventure, combine Grass Wood with a circular walk from Grassington to **Conistone Pie** via **Mastiles Lane**—a quiet route rich in limestone

scenery and sweeping views. Take extra care on wet limestone pavements; the clints and grikes can be slippery and deep in places.

Conclusion:

Grass Wood Nature Reserve and its surrounding limestone pavements offer a deeply immersive and meditative alternative to the Dales' more photographed hotspots. Here, time seems to stretch in the hush of the trees and the stone beneath your feet holds secrets from an ancient sea. Whether you're a curious naturalist, a quiet walker, or a geology lover tracing Earth's frozen history, this is a sanctuary to slow down, listen, and remember that nature is the original storyteller.

Chapter 5: Where to Eat & Drink in the Dales

5.1 Traditional Yorkshire Cuisine

Where Hearty Dales Fare Meets Centuries of Farming Tradition

The Yorkshire Dales is more than a haven for hikers and hill lovers—it's also a region where tradition lives on through food. Long before the modern organic movement or the slow food revolution, the Dales had already perfected the art of hearty, honest meals made with local ingredients. Rooted in centuries of pastoral farming, sheep-rearing, and dairying, traditional Yorkshire cuisine offers a rich taste of the land: warming stews, crumbly cheeses, oatcakes fresh off the griddle, and roasts cooked low and slow in village kitchens. It's simple, robust food, designed to fuel bodies after a day of work—or walking—in the elements. And while you'll find modern interpretations throughout the region, the true heart of Dales cuisine beats strongest in its historic market towns, country pubs, farm tearooms, and community cafés.

Travelers looking to taste the real Yorkshire should seek out spots that serve authentic fare prepared with locally sourced meats, root vegetables, and dairy—all produced in the very landscapes you'll be exploring. Whether you're dipping crusty bread into mutton stew in Hawes or trying a proper Yorkshire curd tart in Reeth, each dish carries the imprint of the region's rugged geography and resilient spirit.

Description:
Traditional Yorkshire cooking is known for being generous, unfussy, and deeply tied to local ingredients. It developed in isolated hill farms and close-knit villages, where seasonal, preserved, and homegrown food formed the basis of daily life. While the best-known export might be the **Yorkshire pudding**, the region's full culinary identity includes rich stews like **lobby** (a mix of meat, root veg, and barley), **Yorkshire parkin** (a sticky ginger cake made with treacle and oats), **game pies**, **rhubarb crumble** (using rhubarb from the nearby Rhubarb Triangle), and **Dales lamb** served with minted gravy.

The Dales also shine in dairy. **Wensleydale cheese**, with its light crumb and gentle tang, is the best-known example. Still handcrafted in Hawes, it's often paired with fruitcake or apple pie—a tradition locals swear by. In tea rooms and farm shops, you'll find **homemade oatcakes**, **fruit scones with clotted cream**, and **butter-rich shortbread** served with **Yorkshire Tea**, a regional staple.

The farm-to-table ethos runs deep, often without using the term. Many inns and eateries grow their own herbs and veg, raise their own livestock, or work directly with neighboring farms and dairies. Traditional Yorkshire cuisine isn't just what's on the plate—it's how it got there: fresh from the field, barn, or bakehouse, often by hand.

Location:
You'll find excellent traditional Yorkshire food throughout the Dales, but some of the most reliable spots are in:

- **Hawes** – home of Wensleydale cheese and many family-run tea rooms
- **Grassington** – known for its characterful pubs and hearty meals
- **Reeth** – traditional dishes served in local inns with scenic views
- **Masham** – offers a strong food market culture and local lamb dishes
- **Malham** – great for cozy cafés and simple, delicious home cooking

Price:

- Traditional main dishes in pubs and inns: **$14–$22 USD**
- Two-course meal in a tearoom or country inn: **$20–$30 USD**
- Local cheese boards or ploughman's lunch: **$12–$18 USD**

- Afternoon tea (with sandwiches, scones, and cakes): **$18–$28 USD**

Opening Hours:

Most eateries in the Dales operate seasonally, with longer hours from **April to October**. Typical hours:

- **Lunch service**: 12:00 PM – 2:30 PM
- **Dinner service**: 6:00 PM – 9:00 PM
- **Tearooms/Cafés**: 10:00 AM – 4:30 PM
- Closed or reduced hours in winter (November–February); check websites or call ahead

Website:

Each establishment has its own site; however, a few resources for traditional Yorkshire cuisine in the Dales include:

- www.yorkshiredales.org.uk/eating-out
- www.realale.org.uk – for alcohol-free local drink pairings like ginger beer or apple juice
- www.wensleydale.co.uk – Wensleydale Creamery in Hawes

Key Features:

- Deep culinary roots in local agriculture and historic village traditions
- Home cooking style: stews, roasts, puddings, and pies
- Emphasis on lamb, beef, root vegetables, dairy, and seasonal fruit
- Strong tea culture with local scones, jams, and cakes
- Community-focused food scenes—family-run tearooms, farmer's markets, and old inns
- Recipes handed down for generations, often with subtle local variations

Visitor Services:

- **Dietary accommodation**: Most places offer vegetarian options; gluten-free choices are available at some cafés and bakeries
- **Children welcome**: Highchairs and children's menus common in pubs and tearooms
- **Reservations**: Recommended for dinner in small villages and on weekends
- **Parking**: Public parking often available nearby; village centres tend to fill early on weekends
- **Locally sourced goods**: Farm shops often sell jams, curds, breads, oatcakes, and cheese to take home

- **Workshops & tastings**: The Wensleydale Creamery and several farm shops offer food demos or tastings seasonally

Contact Address (Example Establishments):

- **The Wensleydale Creamery Visitor Centre**
  Gayle Lane, Hawes, DL8 3RN
  Phone: +44 (0)1969 667664
  Website: www.wensleydale.co.uk

- **The Clarendon Country Pub & Restaurant**
  Hebden, Skipton BD23 5DE
  Phone: +44 (0)1756 752446

- **The King's Arms** (Featured in *All Creatures Great and Small*)
  Askrigg, DL8 3HQ
  Phone: +44 (0)1969 650113

- **The Old School Tearoom**
  Hebden, near Grassington, BD23 5DX
  Phone: +44 (0)1756 752886

Pro tip:
If you're only going to try one thing, make it a **ploughman's lunch**—a classic cold plate featuring bread, cheese (Wensleydale or Swaledale), chutney, salad, and often apple or pickled onions. It's rustic, delicious, and deeply Yorkshire. Pair it with a bottle of locally pressed apple juice or rhubarb cordial for the full Dales taste experience.

Conclusion:
Traditional Yorkshire cuisine is a proud expression of the Dales' heritage, hospitality, and harmony with the land. These dishes aren't just comforting—they're carriers of memory, culture, and community. In an age of quick bites and industrial kitchens, sitting down to a slow-cooked stew, a fresh-baked oatcake, or a wedge of local cheese becomes a way of connecting not only with the place, but with the people and stories that shaped it.

5.2 Tearooms, Bakeries & Coffee Houses

The Heartbeat of Village Life in the Dales

In the Yorkshire Dales, tearooms are more than just places to sip a warm brew—they are the social hubs of village life, the resting posts for weary walkers, and the keepers of centuries-old baking traditions. Whether tucked into stone cottages in hamlets like Kettlewell or set along the cobbled market squares of Grassington or Reeth, these small establishments offer a comforting, time-honoured experience that's rooted in generosity, community, and homemade delights. Alongside them, the growing number of artisan bakeries and independent coffee houses adds a modern twist to the Dales' culinary landscape, blending contemporary tastes with old-fashioned hospitality.

The moment you step inside a Dales tearoom, the aroma of fresh-baked scones, buttery shortbread, and rich fruitcake welcomes you like an old friend. There's always a kettle on the boil, jam bubbling on the stove, and a cake under a glass dome waiting to be sliced. In recent years, the region's café culture has also seen a quiet transformation. Small-batch coffee roasters, plant-based bakeries, and ethically sourced tea specialists have begun to pop up, enriching the local scene while still honouring its roots. Whether you're indulging in an elegant afternoon tea or grabbing a flaky sausage roll and a cappuccino to go, these establishments promise quality, character, and a distinctively Yorkshire sense of place.

Description:

Tearooms in the Yorkshire Dales typically serve a full menu of traditional English bakes, savoury snacks, and homemade meals in cozy, rustic settings. You'll find **fruit scones** served warm with clotted cream and raspberry jam, **Victoria sponge cakes** layered with whipped cream and fresh strawberries, and hearty **Yorkshire curd tarts** made with soft cheese and subtle citrus notes. These classic recipes are often made using ingredients sourced from local farms and gardens, and many tearooms pride themselves on baking everything fresh daily.

On the savoury side, options include **toasted sandwiches, homemade soups, jacket potatoes**, and seasonal quiches. Vegetarian and gluten-free offerings are increasingly common, especially in bakeries with a modern twist. Expect to find **cheese and leek pasties**, **roasted vegetable focaccias**, and **lentil soups** made from scratch.

Artisan bakeries are also gaining prominence, focusing on sourdough breads, wild-fermented pastries, and traditional loaves like **granary, bloomer**, and **oat cob**. You'll also see regional specialties like **Fat Rascals**—a rich cross between a scone and a rock cake, studded with fruit and topped with a cherry-eyed face. Meanwhile, Dales coffee houses are beginning to rival urban cafés with their commitment to specialty beans, espresso craft, and latte artistry, all without losing the friendly warmth the area is known for.

Afternoon tea remains a cherished ritual. Often served on tiered stands with mismatched china, it includes finger sandwiches (such as egg cress, cucumber, or smoked trout), warm scones, jam, cream, and a selection of homemade cakes and biscuits. Some tearooms offer a Dales twist on this classic, featuring local cheese scones, seasonal preserves, and even herbal teas grown in nearby walled gardens.

Location:

Outstanding tearooms, bakeries, and coffee houses are spread across the Dales. Some standout villages and towns include:

- **Grassington** – for its variety of well-established tearooms and new-age cafés
- **Hawes** – home to beloved tea shops serving Wensleydale cheese scones and hearty lunches
- **Settle** – boasts a range of bakeries, cafés, and a strong local food culture
- **Reeth** – scenic views and old-world charm accompany freshly baked treats
- **Leyburn** – a fine stop for family-run coffee houses and pastry shops

- **Skipton** – offers a more cosmopolitan café scene within reach of traditional Dales fare

Price:

- Cream tea (scone, cream, jam, tea): **$6–$10 USD**
- Afternoon tea for one: **$18–$28 USD**
- Artisan coffee with cake or pastry: **$6–$9 USD**
- Sandwich or light lunch: **$8–$14 USD**
- Whole cakes or bread loaves to go: **$6–$20 USD**, depending on item

Opening Hours:
Most tearooms and cafés operate between **9:30 AM and 5:00 PM**, with limited hours in winter months. Few are open in the evening.

- **Summer months (April to October)**: 7 days a week, often from **9:30 AM – 5:00 PM**
- **Winter months (November to February)**: Closed 1–2 days a week, hours often **10:00 AM – 4:00 PM**
- Always check individual websites or call ahead in the low season.

Website:
Each tearoom or café usually maintains a small site or social media page. To explore options and reviews:

- www.yorkshiredales.org.uk/eating-out
- www.visitgrassington.co.uk
- www.yorkshirelife.co.uk – for articles on top bakeries and cafés

Key Features:

- Freshly baked scones, cakes, and breads made daily
- Wide tea selection: black, green, herbal, and locally blended options
- Artisan coffee using single-origin beans and skilled baristas
- Cozy, vintage interiors with wooden beams, mismatched china, and friendly staff
- Locally sourced ingredients used in both sweet and savoury menus
- Some bakeries and coffee houses offer gluten-free, dairy-free, and vegan selections
- Opportunity to buy cakes, jams, and biscuits to take home
- Outdoor seating often available with views of village greens or riverbanks

Visitor Services:

- **Family friendly**: Most venues welcome children and offer highchairs, children's portions, and snacks
- **Dietary options**: Gluten-free, vegan, and dairy-free choices becoming more widely available
- **Wi-Fi**: Available at most modern cafés and coffee houses
- **Parking**: On-street or nearby car parks; larger towns like Settle and Skipton offer more convenient access
- **Restrooms**: Provided onsite; some also have baby-changing facilities
- **Pet friendly**: Several cafés allow dogs, especially those with outdoor seating

Contact Address (Example Establishments):

- **The Bakewell Tearoom**
  Main Street, Grassington, BD23 5AA
  Phone: +44 (0)1756 752856

- **Herriot's Kitchen**
  Market Place, Hawes, DL8 3RD
  Phone: +44 (0)1969 667536

- **The Courtyard Dairy Café**
  near Settle, Austwick, LA2 8AS
  Phone: +44 (0)1729 823291
  Website: www.thecourtyarddairy.co.uk

- **Mill Race Teashop**
  Aysgarth Falls National Park Centre, DL8 3TH
  Phone: +44 (0)1969 663775

- **Three Hares Café**
  Main Street, Sedbergh, LA10 5BL
  Phone: +44 (0)15396 21058
  Known for high-end pastries, sourdough breads, and specialty coffee

Pro tip:
Ask about the **cake of the day** or **seasonal bakes**—many tearooms pride themselves on one-off creations using fruits, herbs, or nuts from local gardens or hedgerows. In summer, look for elderflower drizzle cake or gooseberry tart; in autumn, try plum spice loaf or apple gingerbread.

Conclusion:

Tearooms, bakeries, and coffee houses in the Yorkshire Dales offer more than refreshments—they provide connection, comfort, and a slow, meaningful moment amid the natural grandeur of the landscape. Whether you're winding down after a waterfall hike or beginning your day with a strong cuppa and a warm scone, these spots turn ordinary breaks into cherished rituals. They tell a quiet but compelling story of Yorkshire life—one kettle, one cake, one kind conversation at a time.

5.3 Farm Shops, Cheese Makers & Local Producers

It begins with a scent carried on the wind — the warm, nutty smell of baking bread, the sweet sharpness of apple chutney, or a whiff of sheep's wool and damp grass after morning rain. In the Dales, food doesn't come from distant places. It comes from the barn next door, the field over the hill, or the little stone kitchen down the lane. You don't just eat here — you know where it came from, who made it, and how it changes with the seasons. This is food rooted in place, slow-grown, hand-shaped, and shared with quiet pride.

Where Tradition Still Lives in Every Crumb

The farm shops and cheese makers of the Yorkshire Dales are part of everyday life. They're not attractions made for visitors — though you'll be welcomed like an old friend — but working parts of the land's rhythm. Many shops are small, family-run spaces with shelves made from reclaimed timber, windows that fog with steam in winter, and counters where local kids still spend their pocket money. You'll find rhubarb jams, crab apple jelly, fat links of sausage wrapped in wax paper, and oatcakes stacked beside hand-labeled jars of pickled beetroot. The cheese is often cut right in front of you. The eggs still warm from the coop. Everything smells real — like earth, wood, wool, and flour.

Wensleydale Creamery – The Heart of Dales Cheesemaking

Description: The most iconic food destination in the Yorkshire Dales, Wensleydale Creamery in Hawes has been crafting cheese since 1897. It's where the original Wensleydale — crumbly, tangy, and milky-sweet — is still made by hand. Visitors can explore a cheese-making viewing gallery, enjoy guided tastings, and visit the on-site cheese shop and café offering over 20 varieties of local cheese.

Location: Gayle Lane, Hawes, North Yorkshire, DL8 3RN

Price: Cheese tasting experience: approx. $5 USD. Cheese wedges and hampers: $6–$25 USD depending on size and selection.

Key Features: Authentic Wensleydale production, cheese museum, viewing gallery, artisan shop, and family-friendly café with sweeping views of the Dales.

Visitor Services: Wheelchair accessible, child-friendly, free parking, restrooms, baby changing facilities, café serving local dishes, seasonal events.

Contact Address: Phone: +44 (0)1969 667664

Website: www.wensleydale.co.uk

Curlew Dairy – Raw Milk Cheese from a Wild Hilltop Farm

Description: Just outside Reeth, Curlew Dairy is a small artisan creamery making cheese entirely by hand from raw milk. Their signature cheese, "Old Roan," is rich, creamy, and deeply tied to the farm's meadow-fed cows. Visits are quiet, personal, and often led by the cheesemaker herself. It's not fancy — it's genuine.

Location: Hudswell, Richmond, North Yorkshire, DL11 6BH

Price: Cheese purchases: $8–$18 USD per wedge. No charge for farm visits, but call ahead.

Key Features: Organic raw milk cheese, single herd production, sustainable farming, handmade batches, personal farm visits.

Visitor Services: Limited parking, no café or facilities, rustic site best for mobile guests, call ahead for seasonal availability.

Contact Address: Email: curlewdairy@gmail.com

Website: www.curlewdairy.co.uk

The Home Farmer – Milk on Tap and More
Description: Near Aysgarth, The Home Farmer offers a fresh milk vending machine, cheeses, butter, cream, and local produce from their own cows and neighboring farms. It's a simple, self-serve setup that works on honesty and community spirit. Children love the "milkshake mix" options, and the views over Wensleydale are pure postcard.

Location: Aysgarth, Leyburn, North Yorkshire, DL8 3AQ

Price: Fresh milk: $1.50 USD per litre. Cheese and butter from $3–$12 USD.

Key Features: Vending machine for raw and pasteurized milk, farm-fresh produce, self-service dairy hut, scenic setting, locally made butter and cream.

Visitor Services: Free parking, family-friendly, outdoor benches, seasonal local events, 24/7 access to vending.

Contact Address: Phone: +44 (0)1969 663299

Website: www.thehomefarmer.co.uk

Town End Farm Shop – Butchery, Deli & Field-Fresh Veg
Description: Sitting just outside Malham, Town End is a polished but still deeply local farm shop offering home-reared meats, hand-tied sausages, Yorkshire cheeses, and a proper café with views of sheep-filled fields. It's a one-stop shop for high-quality, real Dales food and the sort of place where every pie has a story behind it.

Location: Airton, Skipton, North Yorkshire, BD23 4BE

Price: Deli items from $5 USD. Full café meals from $10–$22 USD. Meat cuts vary: approx. $6–$15 USD per lb.

Key Features: On-site butchery, local cheese counter, seasonal produce, café with daily specials, traditional puddings and cakes.

Visitor Services: Ample parking, clean toilets, picnic areas, accessible entrance, dog-friendly outside, shop and café open daily.

Contact Address: Phone: +44 (0)1756 748481

Website: www.townendfarmshop.co.uk

Reeth Community Shop – The Local Spirit in One Room
 Description: In the heart of Swaledale, Reeth's village shop is entirely community-run and brimming with produce from dozens of local makers. From honeys and chutneys to cakes, breads, and handmade crafts, it's the soul of the Dales wrapped in a single warm, bustling room. All profits go back into local services.

Location: Reeth, Richmond, North Yorkshire, DL11 6SP

Price: Local products range from $2–$20 USD depending on type and size.

Key Features: Wide selection of local food producers, community-owned and operated, homemade cakes and sweets, focus on local crafts and ethical goods.

Visitor Services: Nearby parking, ATM, post office, walking distance to pubs and cafés, open seven days a week.

Contact Address: Phone: +44 (0)1748 884759

Website: www.reethcommunityshop.co.uk

Pro tip: Always keep a few coins or small bills with you. Many honesty boxes — especially in remote villages or outside little barns — don't take cards. That £2 jar of jam, made from someone's backyard berries, might be the best souvenir you bring home.

Conclusion:
 Food in the Dales isn't just about filling your belly. It's about slowing down, meeting the people behind the counter, and tasting something made with care and place. In a world of fast choices and plastic packaging, the simple pleasure of a crumbly cheese, a warm pie, or a bottle of raw milk from just over the hill is something rare. And here, in these soft, rolling hills, it's still right at your fingertips.

5.4 Organic Cafés & Wholefood Kitchens

The Yorkshire Dales aren't just home to hearty stews and traditional meat pies. Nestled among the limestone villages and misty hills are a growing number of organic cafés and wholefood kitchens that nourish the body as much as the soul. These eateries are quietly redefining what it means to eat well in the countryside — crafting meals from scratch, sourcing ingredients directly from local farms, and creating warm, welcoming spaces that feel more like home than restaurants. For the wellness traveler, the plant-based eater, or anyone seeking mindful, wholesome dining, these are havens worth discovering.

From Farm to Fork — With Heart in Every Bite
These cafés don't just slap "organic" on a label. They live and breathe it. Most grow their own produce or have deep relationships with neighboring farms. Herbs come from kitchen gardens, salads are picked that morning, and menus change with the seasons. You'll find turmeric lattes, slow-roasted beetroot hummus, sprouted grain bread, and homemade kombucha served with the same care as a fine tea. But it's never pretentious. You'll sip your herbal brew beside a sheepdog napping by the fire or chat with the owner while she bakes sourdough behind the counter.

The Retreat Tearoom & Bistro – A Tranquil Plant-Based Escape

Description: Tucked away in the peaceful village of Grassington, The Retreat is a vegetarian and mostly vegan café that feels more like a sanctuary than a shop. With handmade wooden tables, soft acoustic music, and windows that frame views of rolling hills, it's a place to slow down and savor. The kitchen uses entirely organic, locally sourced ingredients to create vibrant salads, hearty grain bowls, soups, and raw desserts. Their turmeric chai, served with oat milk, is a favorite among hikers and healers alike.

Location: 1 Main Street, Grassington, Skipton, North Yorkshire, BD23 5AA

Price: Mains from $9–$16 USD. Organic drinks and smoothies from $3–$6 USD. Cakes and snacks from $3 USD.

Key Features: 100% vegetarian, organic and vegan-friendly, gluten-free options, cozy interior, dog-friendly courtyard, takeaway available.

Visitor Services: Indoor and outdoor seating, toilets, child-friendly, wheel-accessible entrance, free Wi-Fi, wellness products and local crafts for sale.

Contact Address: Phone: +44 (0)1756 752822

Website: www.retreatcafebistro.com

The Health Barn – Organic Food in the Heart of a Working Farm

Description: Located on the edge of Settle, The Health Barn is a wholefood kitchen and farm shop housed in a converted barn overlooking lush pastures. Their menu changes daily based on what's in season — think organic lentil curry, sprouted chickpea wraps, spinach and walnut pesto pasta, and fresh juices made to order. Their commitment to zero waste is impressive, with compostable packaging and no single-use plastics in sight.

Location: Langcliffe Hall Farm, Settle, North Yorkshire, BD24 9NF

Price: Meals from $8–$14 USD. Cold-pressed juices and wellness shots from $4–$6 USD.

Key Features: Farm-to-table dishes, plant-based menu, homemade granolas, kombucha on tap, refill station for organic pantry staples, eco-gift shop.

Visitor Services: Ample parking, accessible toilets, kid's corner, stroller-friendly paths, seasonal workshops (fermentation, bread baking, herbalism).

Contact Address: Phone: +44 (0)1729 822555

Website: www.thehealthbarn.co.uk

Forage – Small, Honest, and Rooted in Nature

Description: Sitting quietly on the outskirts of Ilkley, Forage is a tiny, heartfelt café run by two sisters who believe food should be simple, beautiful, and healing. They serve just a handful of dishes a day — such as roasted root vegetables over quinoa with tahini drizzle, or their signature green soup with nettle, kale, and sweet potato. The kitchen also runs on a "closed-loop" system, meaning all food waste goes back to compost or animal feed on nearby farms.

Location: 3 Ash Grove, Ilkley, West Yorkshire, LS29 8EP

Price: Daily plate: $10 USD. Soups: $6 USD. Organic teas and herbals: $3 USD.

Key Features: Minimalist interior, rotating daily menus, medicinal teas, foraged ingredients, sustainability-focused, community-supported.

Visitor Services: Very limited seating (mostly takeaway), eco-packaging, walking distance from Ilkley rail station, dog treats and water bowls outside.

Contact Address: Instagram DM only (@forageilkley) — no phone line.

Website: www.forageilkley.co.uk

Elly's Wholefoods – Where Wellness Meets Comfort

Description: Elly's in Richmond blends the feel of a deli, health food store, and warm café. It's especially popular with walkers and cyclists passing through, offering hearty and healthy dishes like black bean chili with cornbread, cashew cheese toasties, and homemade apple cider vinegar tonics. The interior features big armchairs, reclaimed wooden floors, and jars of house-blended teas. Elly, a trained nutritionist, often pops out of the kitchen to chat about recipes and healing foods.

Location: 11 Frenchgate, Richmond, North Yorkshire, DL10 7AE

Price: Hot meals from $9–$15 USD. Tonics and elixirs from $3 USD. Superfood smoothies and bowls from $5–$9 USD.

Key Features: Organic, wholefood-based meals, nutritional guidance, refill section for grains and herbs, takeaway freezer meals, events and tastings.

Visitor Services: Indoor seating, accessible entry, book nook for children, workshops on natural wellness and gut health, open Monday–Saturday.

Contact Address: Phone: +44 (0)1748 850207

Website: www.ellyswholefoods.co.uk

The Courtyard Dairy Café – Cheese Meets Wholegrain Warmth
Description: Known nationally for its award-winning cheeses, The Courtyard Dairy also runs a small café with a surprising emphasis on balanced, nourishing meals. Though not fully vegetarian, their dishes include plenty of meat-free, wholefood-forward options. Think heritage grain salads, roasted squash with black garlic, and farmhouse breads paired with cheese from just yards away. The café also offers fermented drinks and slow-brewed herbal infusions from local growers.

Location: A65, near Austwick, North Yorkshire, LA2 8AS

Price: Meals from $10–$18 USD. Cheese platters from $15 USD. Herbal teas and drinks from $3–$5 USD.

Key Features: Artisan café connected to world-famous cheese shop, thoughtful sourcing, balance of indulgence and health, hill views from glass wall seating.

Visitor Services: Parking, toilets, shop, cheese counter, educational boards, tours available with advance booking.

Contact Address: Phone: +44 (0)15242 410202

Website: www.thecourtyarddairy.co.uk

Pro tip: Many of these cafés close early — around 4 or 5 p.m. — and some only open Thursday to Sunday, especially in winter. Always check ahead, and don't be surprised if the best dish is "what's left" on the board when you arrive near closing.

Conclusion:
Eating organically in the Yorkshire Dales isn't a trend — it's a quiet return to what this land has always done best: growing real food, in real soil, with real care. These wholefood kitchens and cafés are deeply personal places where the people cooking and serving also sow, gather, and believe in what they feed you. They're places where your meal might begin in a hedgerow and end in a handmade bowl. And in a world rushing faster every day, they remind you that sometimes, the most nourishing thing isn't just the food — it's the peace and purpose behind it.

Chapter 6: Towns, Villages & Local Life

6.1 Hawes & the Upper Wensleydale Area

Hawes sits cradled in the heart of Upper Wensleydale like a stone-stitched patchwork of time, tradition, and tenacity. It is the highest market town in England, yet it greets visitors with an open warmth that feels distinctly grounded — not just in elevation, but in heritage. This bustling dale settlement is a microcosm of Dale's life: cobbled lanes humming with chatter, ancient inns that serve hearty food, art galleries alongside sheep auctions, and dairies producing the area's most iconic cheese. From its weekly Tuesday market to the footpaths that radiate out toward waterfalls and moorland, Hawes remains unapologetically local and vibrantly alive.

Description:

Hawes is not a place you pass through — it's one you settle into, even if just for an afternoon. Though modest in size, it pulses with community life. The town's rhythm follows age-old cycles: lambing in spring, hay-cutting in summer, sheep shows in autumn, and quiet fireside gatherings in winter. The River Ure splits the town as it flows eastward, while fells rise dramatically around it, offering dramatic walks and photo-worthy views. Even with growing tourism, Hawes has not been overly polished. You'll see muddy boots on café floors, neighbors leaning over garden walls for a chat, and farmers arriving at the auction mart still dusted in hay.

Location:
Hawes lies in Upper Wensleydale, North Yorkshire, within the Yorkshire Dales National Park. It sits just off the A684, approximately 16 miles west of Leyburn and 13 miles east of Sedbergh. The closest train station is Garsdale, about 6 miles away, accessible via the Settle–Carlisle Line. Buses connect Hawes to Richmond, Leyburn, and Ingleton (services are limited on Sundays and holidays).

Key Features:
Hawes offers an unusually rich blend of heritage and daily life. Its key features include:

The Wensleydale Creamery: World-famous for producing Wensleydale cheese, this working creamery is both a visitor attraction and a living slice of local food culture. There's a viewing gallery to watch cheese-making, tasting rooms, and a shop with over 20 varieties of local cheese. Cheese-making demonstrations run daily (except Sundays).

Hardraw Force: Just north of Hawes lies England's highest single-drop waterfall above ground. Reached through the 13th-century Green Dragon Inn, the waterfall is set in a wooded gorge and offers a peaceful retreat in all seasons.

The Dales Countryside Museum: Located in the former railway station, this museum provides a comprehensive look into Dales history — from prehistoric settlers and Viking influences to farming tools, crafts, and the rise of tourism.

The Tuesday Market: Still a cornerstone of Hawes' weekly rhythm, the open-air market features local produce, handmade goods, vintage finds, and tools. The auction mart nearby hosts livestock sales that draw both locals and curious travelers.

Village Shops & Galleries: From Outhwaite Ropemakers (still operating Victorian looms) to photography galleries, woodturning studios, and sweet shops, Hawes is rich with locally run businesses and makers.

Visitor Services:
Hawes is well-equipped for travelers without losing its intimate feel. Services include:

- **Public Toilets:** Located at the Dales Countryside Museum and the main car park.

- **Parking:** Large pay-and-display car parks are situated near the market square and museum.
- **Tourist Information Centre:** Inside the museum building, offering maps, brochures, and walking advice.
- **Public Transport:** Limited bus services — check DalesBus timetables for up-to-date routes.
- **Medical:** A local GP surgery and pharmacy are available near the market square.
- **Wi-Fi & Connectivity:** Mobile signals can be patchy; several cafés offer free Wi-Fi.

Price:
Entry to the Dales Countryside Museum: $6 USD for adults, $4 USD for children.
Cheese-making demonstrations at Wensleydale Creamery: $5 USD (includes tasting).
Hardraw Force entry (via Green Dragon Inn): $4 USD per person.
Accommodation ranges from $60–$150 USD per night for B&Bs and inns.
Local cafés and tearooms offer meals from $8–$14 USD.

Contact Address:
Dales Countryside Museum: Station Yard, Hawes, DL8 3NT
Phone: +44 (0)1969 666210
Website: www.dalescountrysidemuseum.org.uk

Wensleydale Creamery: Gayle Lane, Hawes, DL8 3RN
Phone: +44 (0)1969 667664
Website: www.wensleydale.co.uk

Website:
General visitor information can be found at: www.yorkshiredales.org.uk/places/hawes

Local Life:
Though Hawes welcomes thousands of visitors each year, its core is deeply resident-driven. Children walk to the local primary school in wellies, farm dogs nap outside the co-op, and the community hall hosts everything from ceilidhs to crafts fairs. Seasonal rhythms still shape everyday life — be it the summer hay harvest or winter feeding rounds. Hawes also supports a growing group of creative newcomers — potters, weavers, and photographers who have chosen this remote beauty as their muse.

Traditional Celebrations:
In June, Hawes hosts the Swaledale Festival, a two-week celebration of classical music and arts with events across the region. The Hawes Gala Day in summer and the Yuletide Festival in December are packed with local stalls, lantern walks, and children's

performances. Sheepdog trials, fell races, and village shows dot the calendar, offering travelers insight into a lifestyle still anchored in place and people.

Walks & Footpaths:

From the center of Hawes, several walking routes unfold in all directions. The Pennine Way slices through town, while circular paths lead to Gayle, Burtersett, and Aysgill Force. The footpath to Hardraw via Sedbusk is a quiet alternative to the main road, offering streamside views and limestone scars. The walk to Great Shunner Fell, the third-highest peak in the Dales, starts just outside town and is a challenging but rewarding ascent.

Where to Stay & Eat:

Hawes is rich in family-run inns and warm tearooms. Popular options include the White Hart Inn, which offers traditional meals and historic charm, and the Board Inn, where hearty Dales portions are standard. For daytime fare, cafés like Laburnum House and The Town Foot are known for their soups, scones, and cheerful atmosphere. Organic and vegetarian offerings are limited but growing, with some cafés now offering plant-based stews and oat milk options.

Conclusion:

Hawes is more than just a postcard-perfect market town. It's a living, breathing piece of Yorkshire — a place where cheese is still made by hand, dialects carry echoes of Norse heritage, and life is measured in seasons, not screens. For visitors, it offers a rare glimpse into a way of life that still prizes neighborliness, hard work, and landscape as teacher and companion. To walk through Hawes is to walk through centuries of resilience, craftsmanship, and unfiltered beauty — a cornerstone of Upper Wensleydale's enduring soul.

6.2 Grassington & Wharfedale Villages

Tucked into the limestone-rich embrace of Upper Wharfedale, Grassington and its surrounding villages offer a gentler, sun-warmed face of the Yorkshire Dales. With its honey-hued stone cottages, winding alleys, and lively arts community, Grassington blends timeless rural charm with a surprisingly modern cultural heartbeat. Just a short walk or drive from this hub lie smaller villages — Linton, Hebden, Burnsall, and Thorpe — each one a postcard come to life, quietly maintaining customs shaped by centuries of Dales living. Together, these communities form a richly textured portrait of Wharfedale life: part pastoral, part creative, entirely grounded.

Description:
  Grassington feels like a village in bloom. Its cobbled market square, flanked by independent shops, galleries, and cafés, hums with a slow but steady rhythm. There's

always something happening here — a heritage trail walk, a local play, an art opening. Despite its modest size, Grassington plays a starring role in local life, with a population proud of its culture, history, and involvement in preserving the spirit of the Dales. The surrounding villages — each distinct in character — offer peaceful alternatives, ideal for walking holidays, gentle exploration, and slow travel. Linton is known for its graceful arched bridge and 12th-century church. Hebden offers stepping stones across the river and quiet lanes perfect for sketching. Burnsall lies beneath a wide sweep of moorland, its riverbank popular with paddlers and picnickers. Thorpe, tiny and serene, is a hidden gem for those seeking true seclusion.

Location:
Grassington is situated in Upper Wharfedale, North Yorkshire, within the boundaries of the Yorkshire Dales National Park. It lies about 9 miles north of Skipton and 12 miles south of Kettlewell. The nearest train station is in Skipton, from where buses (including the scenic DalesBus) travel to Grassington and other villages. Roads in and out are narrow and winding but passable year-round.

Key Features:

Grassington Market Square: This lively heart of the village has hosted markets since medieval times. Today it's lined with tearooms, local shops, and seasonal events such as Christmas markets and summer festivals. The square is also a starting point for several heritage trails.

Grassington Folk Museum: Located in a 17th-century building, this small but deeply informative museum tells the story of the area's social, agricultural, and lead mining history. Exhibits range from spinning wheels to Victorian schoolrooms.

Linton Falls & River Walks: Just a 10-minute walk from the square, the river tumbles over limestone ledges at Linton Falls. Footpaths along the riverbank connect Grassington with Linton and Hebden, offering some of the most scenic, accessible rambles in the area.

The Old Hall in Linton: Often considered one of the oldest continuously inhabited houses in Yorkshire, this medieval manor turned private residence showcases the region's layered history. While not open to the public, it's visible from nearby paths and remains a key heritage landmark.

Burnsall Bridge & Church: This elegant five-arched bridge spans the River Wharfe and has become one of Wharfedale's most photographed spots. The nearby St Wilfrid's Church, dating to the 1100s, holds medieval woodwork and intriguing grave carvings.

Grass Wood Nature Reserve: Above Grassington lies this ancient limestone woodland, rich in biodiversity. It's a designated Site of Special Scientific Interest, offering quiet trails, spring wildflowers, and glimpses of roe deer and woodpeckers.

Visitor Services:

Grassington serves as a well-equipped hub for the surrounding villages. Services include:

- **Public Toilets:** Available at the National Park Centre and in the main car park.
- **Parking:** Pay-and-display car parks on Hebden Road and the National Park Centre.
- **Tourist Information:** Located inside the Grassington National Park Centre, offering maps, trail info, and event details.
- **Buses:** Regular services run from Skipton to Grassington; seasonal buses connect with Hebden, Burnsall, and Kettlewell.
- **Mobile Signal & Wi-Fi:** Signal is generally good in Grassington but weaker in smaller villages. Some cafés offer free Wi-Fi.
- **Medical Services:** The nearest GP and pharmacy are in Grassington; hospitals are in Skipton and Harrogate.

Price:

Grassington Folk Museum: Admission is donation-based (suggested $3–$5 USD).
Parking in Grassington: Around $3–$6 USD per day.
Average meal in cafés and tearooms: $10–$16 USD.
Local accommodations range from $70 to $160 USD per night depending on season and amenities.

Contact Address:

Grassington National Park Centre: Hebden Road, Grassington, BD23 5LB
Phone: +44 (0)1756 751690
Website: www.yorkshiredales.org.uk

Grassington Folk Museum: The Square, Grassington, BD23 5AQ
Phone: +44 (0)1756 753445
Website: www.grassingtonfolkmuseum.org.uk

Website:

General info on the area and surrounding villages: www.yorkshiredales.org.uk/places/grassington

Local Life:

Unlike many rural destinations, Grassington has maintained a healthy balance between tourism and community life. The village has a primary school, churches, a medical centre, and a full calendar of local events. Its arts scene is particularly strong, thanks to the legacy of writers, musicians, and painters who've called the Dales home. Summer sees artists' open studios and literary walks; winter brings the Dickensian Festival, when the streets fill with costumed locals, carolers, and stalls selling handmade crafts.

The surrounding villages have fewer amenities but richer quiet. In Linton, farming families have held the same plots for generations. Hebden and Thorpe offer silence broken only by birdsong and the occasional tractor. Burnsall's riverbank is a favorite family picnic spot, while its primary school still hosts Maypole dancing on the green.

Traditional Celebrations:
Grassington's Dickensian Festival, held over two weekends in December, transforms the town into a Victorian wonderland with street performances, mulled juice, traditional games, and charity stalls. The Grassington Festival in June is a ten-day celebration of music, art, and performance that attracts national talent while showcasing local voices. Other recurring events include scarecrow trails, agricultural shows, and well-dressing ceremonies in nearby Linton.

Walks & Footpaths:
This part of Wharfedale is among the most walkable in the Dales. Short, scenic routes include the circular path from Grassington to Linton and Hebden along the River Wharfe, with stepping stones and bird hides en route. More strenuous hikes include the 9-mile loop to Conistone Dib — a narrow limestone gorge — or the ascent to Bare House and beyond for panoramic dale views. The Dales Way also passes through Burnsall and Grassington, offering extended walking opportunities.

Where to Stay & Eat:
Grassington offers characterful lodging, such as Ashfield House (4-star, stylish country décor) and The Black Horse Hotel (a historic coaching inn with hearty meals). Linton has The Fountaine Inn, a scenic riverside inn known for local dishes and calm atmosphere. Hebden and Burnsall have fewer beds but provide peaceful, family-run guesthouses. Dining options in Grassington include The Retreat Tearoom, known for vegetarian lunches and Yorkshire rarebit, and The Foresters Arms, a traditional spot for soups, roast dinners, and puddings. Organic and wholefood choices are increasingly available, especially during festival periods.

Conclusion:
Grassington and the Wharfedale villages together offer a layered experience of Dale's life: one part cultural exploration, one part natural immersion. Whether you're wandering through an art gallery, watching trout in the River Wharfe, or sipping tea in a centuries-old parlour, every moment feels connected to land and legacy. These villages

remind visitors that beauty and meaning often live in the quieter corners — not just in grand landscapes, but in shared stories, open gates, and the warmth of a well-tended hearth.

6.3 Reeth & Swaledale Hamlets

Reeth, set like a polished stone at the meeting of Swaledale's two rivers—the Arkle and the Swale—is the understated jewel of the northern Dales. This village, with its spacious green and sweeping upland views, functions as the cultural and practical heart of upper Swaledale. A walk around its triangular green might take only minutes, but the surrounding hamlets—Healaugh, Grinton, Low Row, and Muker—extend the experience deep into one of the Dales' wildest, most characterful valleys. Each community is shaped by its legacy of lead mining, handcrafting, hill farming, and a resilient connection to land, tradition, and community.

Description:
Reeth itself is quietly lively. There's a sense of independence here: in its locally run shops, its galleries, and in the pace of life that still bows to the rhythm of seasons and sheep. The green is expansive, bordered by inns, cafés, and cottages. Cyclists and walkers often gather here, but few rush. Reeth's deep roots lie in centuries of farming and mining, and though the lead seams have long since dried up, the pride in that heritage remains visible everywhere—from museums to dry stone walls. Each nearby hamlet has a different flavor: Healaugh is tiny and utterly peaceful; Grinton boasts a striking church and one of the oldest bridges in Swaledale; Low Row offers elevated views and hidden lanes; Muker is the heart of hay meadow country, rich in traditional crafts and botany.

Location:
Reeth lies in the heart of Swaledale, North Yorkshire, within the northern section of the Yorkshire Dales National Park. It's about 12 miles west of Richmond via the B6270, a scenic but narrow road that winds through the dale. Public transport is limited but includes seasonal DalesBus services from Richmond and Leyburn. Reeth is well connected by footpaths, bridleways, and cycling routes to nearby villages.

Key Features:

Reeth Village Green: The defining centerpiece of the village, surrounded by cafés, craft shops, and historic pubs. Informal gatherings, markets, and community events often take place here.

Swaledale Museum: A compact but rich museum tucked behind the green, it offers hands-on exhibits on the area's lead mining, knitting, domestic life, and agriculture. Run by local volunteers, it reflects community pride and archival care.

The Grinton Church of St Andrew: Known locally as "The Cathedral of the Dales", this beautiful 12th-century church was the end point of the "corpse way," a centuries-old funeral route from Keld. Inside, you'll find ancient woodwork and a peaceful atmosphere.

Reeth Dales Centre: Located at the edge of the village, this serves as a visitor information hub with a café, art gallery, and outdoor gear shop. It's a popular starting point for circular walks around Reeth and into Arkengarthdale.

Muker's Hay Meadows: Just up-dale from Reeth, Muker is home to some of the UK's best-preserved traditional hay meadows. In late spring and early summer, these meadows burst into bloom, filled with rare native flowers like wood cranesbill and yellow rattle.

Low Row's Redmire Scar Walk: This gentle hillside path gives elevated views over the dale, ideal for sunrise or dusk walks. Low Row is also dotted with old field barns and steep pastures that reflect centuries of upland farming.

Visitor Services:
Despite its small size, Reeth is well-prepared to support visitors:

- **Public Toilets:** Located by the green and at the Dales Centre.
- **Parking:** Ample pay-and-display parking around the village green.
- **Tourist Information:** Available at the Reeth Dales Centre.
- **Shops:** Several craft stores, a bakery, a small grocery shop, and post office.
- **Wi-Fi & Mobile:** Patchy signal in some hamlets; Reeth has reasonable reception and some Wi-Fi access points.
- **Bus Access:** Limited year-round service from Richmond, expanded during weekends and summer via DalesBus.
- **Medical Services:** Nearest GP is in Reeth; the closest hospitals are in Richmond and Northallerton.

Price:
Swaledale Museum: Entry suggested donation around $4–$6 USD.
Meals at Reeth cafés and inns: $9–$15 USD on average.
Accommodation in Reeth and nearby hamlets: $80–$150 USD per night depending on season and amenities.
Parking: Daily rates around $3–$5 USD.

Contact Address:
Swaledale Museum: The Hill, Reeth, Richmond, DL11 6TB
Phone: +44 (0)1748 884118
Website: www.swaledalemuseum.org

Reeth Dales Centre: Silver Street, Reeth, DL11 6SP
Phone: +44 (0)1748 884059
Website: www.yorkshiredales.org.uk/visit/dales-centres

Website:
Village and area info: www.reeth.org and www.yorkshiredales.org.uk

Local Life:
Reeth remains a working village. Hill farming defines the rhythms of life, particularly in lambing season and at harvest time. While tourism supports many businesses, much of the community's resilience lies in its self-sufficiency. Local events like the Swaledale Festival — a music and arts festival held in late May and early June — bring a burst of

creativity and connectivity to the dale. In winter, the village slows to a quiet hum, with roaring fires, storytelling nights at the pub, and knitters gathered in community halls.

Healaugh and Low Row maintain a particularly local pace, often with unmanned honesty boxes selling jams or handmade items along fences. Muker, despite its popularity during wildflower season, remains rooted in farming life and textile traditions. Grinton's pub and church continue to serve as both spiritual and social centers for the area.

Crafts & Markets:
This part of Swaledale is known for hand-knitting and textile work, and you'll find handmade woollens in local shops or for sale during craft fairs. Muker has a tiny craft shop focused on Dales wool products. Reeth's Hudson House and Silver Street Studios host artist workshops, often open to the public. Weekend markets, especially in warmer months, bring local produce, handmade soap, and home-baked goods to the green.

Walks & Outdoor Exploration:
Numerous circular walks radiate from Reeth, ranging from 2-mile riverside strolls to 12-mile upland hikes over Fremington Edge. The Old Gang Smelt Mill ruins offer a dramatic glimpse into the industrial past, while Calver Hill and Harkerside Moor provide wide-sky panoramas. The Coast-to-Coast path and Swale Trail (a family-friendly cycling route) also pass nearby. For less strenuous activity, the meadows and riverside near Muker offer accessible paths with interpretive signs.

Where to Stay & Eat:
Reeth offers a handful of character-rich inns like The Burgoyne (upscale country hotel with excellent valley views) and The Buck Hotel (traditional pub-style rooms with hearty dinners). Self-catering cottages and B&Bs are available in all surrounding hamlets, often with stone-flagged floors, exposed beams, and open hearths. Dining is simple, local, and satisfying. Try the Two Dales Bakery in Reeth for fresh breads and scones, or head to Grinton's Bridge Inn for homely Yorkshire stews, root vegetable plates, and rich puddings. Tea shops and cafés offer seasonal specials and home-baked options. Many cater to vegetarians and offer plant-based selections on request.

Conclusion:
Reeth and its Swaledale neighbors form a tapestry of village life that is intimate, enduring, and fiercely proud. While walkers and photographers may first be drawn by the raw beauty of the dale — its fells, rivers, and stone barns — they often stay for the warmth of these communities and the sense of time well spent. Whether watching sheep descend a hillside trail at dusk or sharing a simple supper after a long walk, life in this corner of the Dales is best measured not in miles but in moments.

6.4 Settle, Malham & Southern Dales TownsHardraw Force & the Pennine Hills

Settle and Malham, tucked into the craggy limestone folds of the southern Yorkshire Dales, offer a contrast to the upland dales of the north: here the landscape feels more carved than rolling, more dramatically vertical than gently pastoral. The towns and villages of the southern Dales—Settle, Malham, Giggleswick, and nearby hamlets like Langcliffe and Stainforth—serve as gateways to iconic geological formations, extraordinary walking country, and an active local life shaped by both deep tradition and thoughtful innovation. This is where the Dales' ancient limestone meets contemporary creativity, and where you'll find both a fossil-rich gorge and an organic coffee roaster within a few miles of each other.

Description:

Settle is the practical hub of this part of the Dales, a handsome market town nestled along the River Ribble and framed by limestone cliffs and green hillsides. With its historic market square, weekly stalls, small shops, and railway heritage, Settle manages to feel both lived-in and quietly progressive. Art galleries, wholefood cafés, and secondhand bookshops reflect a creative, socially engaged local population.

Just a short drive northeast lies Malham, smaller in size but dramatically large in character. Surrounded by some of the most astonishing natural features in the entire National Park, Malham is a destination for geologists, photographers, and hillwalkers alike. The village itself is charming and centered on a few stone cottages, a tearoom or two, and a popular visitor centre—but it's the surrounding landscape that steals the show.

Nearby villages like Giggleswick and Stainforth bring added texture to this area. Giggleswick is known for its fine school and beautiful chapel, while Langcliffe's mill ruins hint at the region's industrial past. The Ribble Valley, which threads through this part of the park, gives life to riverside walks, deep wooded valleys, and a sense of lushness not always found elsewhere in the Dales.

Location:

Settle is located in the southwestern edge of the Yorkshire Dales National Park, about 25 miles northwest of Skipton and easily accessible via the A65. The Settle-Carlisle Railway connects it to Leeds and Carlisle with one of England's most scenic train routes. Malham is about 6 miles northeast of Settle, reached via a narrow but well-maintained country road. Public transportation includes buses from Settle to Malham during the tourist season.

Key Features:

Settle Market Square: The town's beating heart, featuring a weekly Tuesday market that dates back to 1249. You'll find local produce, crafts, baked goods, plants, and antique items.

Settle-Carlisle Railway Station: A picturesque and functioning historic railway with regular steam train excursions. The station itself is a small museum and a popular photo spot.

The Folly Museum: A 17th-century house turned into a heritage centre that explores local life, architecture, and industry. Family-friendly and engaging, with exhibits that rotate seasonally.

Victoria Hall: England's oldest surviving music hall, now used for film nights, live performances, and community events. Offers a delightful window into Settle's Victorian social life.

Malham Cove: A vast curved limestone amphitheatre carved by glacial meltwaters. A short but steep walk leads up to the top of the cove, where you can tread carefully across a surreal limestone pavement.

Gordale Scar: Just beyond Malham, this towering gorge cuts through the hills with dramatic cliffs and waterfalls. It's a short walk from the road, but offers a moment of awe that feels almost alpine.

Janet's Foss: A picturesque waterfall nestled in ancient woodland, named after a local fairy of legend. It's a peaceful and family-friendly spot with picnic potential and wild swimming for the brave.

Stainforth Force: A stepped cascade near the village of Stainforth, known for the annual salmon leap in autumn. Accessible from the Ribble Way footpath and especially popular with photographers.

Visitor Services:
This southern section of the Dales offers excellent visitor support, especially in Settle and Malham:

- **Public Toilets:** Available at Settle's main car park and near the Malham National Park Centre.
- **Parking:** Settle has several car parks; Malham has limited spaces, best arrived early or off-peak.
- **Tourist Information:** Settle's TIC is in The Folly; Malham has a well-staffed National Park Visitor Centre.
- **Shops:** Settle offers grocery stores, outdoor gear outlets, art galleries, and bookshops. Malham has smaller shops focused on hikers and visitors.
- **Wi-Fi & Mobile:** Good in Settle; more limited in Malham and surrounding countryside.
- **Bus & Train Access:** Settle has regular train service; buses to Malham run mostly in summer.
- **Medical Services:** Settle hosts a small medical centre and pharmacy; nearest hospital is in Skipton.

Price:
The Folly Museum: Approx. $5 USD entry.
Malham National Park Centre: Free to enter; parking $6–$8 USD/day.

Meals at Settle cafés: $10–$18 USD.
Train fares on the Settle-Carlisle line: $15–$25 USD depending on route.
Lodging: From $85–$170 USD/night depending on location and amenities.

Contact Address:
The Folly, Victoria Street, Settle BD24 9EY
Phone: +44 (0)1729 822893
Website: www.ncbpt.org.uk/folly

Malham National Park Centre, Chapel Gate, Malham, BD23 4DA
Phone: +44 (0)1729 833200
Website: www.yorkshiredales.org.uk

Website:
www.settle.org.uk and www.malhamdale.com

Local Life:
Settle is a working town with a strong community identity. Weekly markets remain essential, not just as tourist draws but as gathering points for locals. Creative energy infuses the town—musicians, woodworkers, and visual artists live and exhibit here. Annual events like the Settle Stories Festival and the Flowerpot Festival (featuring whimsical people-shaped plant pots throughout the town) highlight this blend of tradition and modern playfulness.

Malham, despite its tourism focus, retains a deep connection to farming and the land. Shepherds still guide their flocks across high pastures, and many cottages belong to families who've lived in the village for generations. As part of the Dales' sustainable tourism efforts, Malham's footpaths are well-managed, its meadows protected, and its visitor flow monitored carefully to prevent erosion.

Giggleswick offers a quieter, more residential feel, but also boasts one of the region's architectural gems: the Giggleswick Chapel, with its copper dome and stunning Arts & Crafts interior. This part of the Dales feels both spiritual and scholarly, grounded in nature and education alike.

Crafts & Markets:
Settle hosts a wide range of local crafters—ceramics, textiles, woodwork, and landscape art dominate the shopfronts around the square. Don't miss Gallery on the Green, claimed to be the world's smallest art gallery, housed in a phone box. Pop-up craft markets, especially in spring and summer, feature local cheesemakers, herbal products, jams, woollens, and hand-bound books.

Walks & Outdoor Exploration:
This area is a walker's dream. The Malham Landscape Trail offers a circular hike linking Janet's Foss, Gordale Scar, and Malham Cove—about 5 miles of dramatic scenery and rich flora. The Pennine Way passes through Malham, drawing long-distance walkers. In Settle, the Ribble Way and Dales High Way both begin or pass through town, and shorter circular walks explore the limestone crags and wooded valleys.

Where to Stay & Eat:
Settle has everything from coaching inns to boutique B&Bs. The Golden Lion Hotel and Falcon Manor offer historic charm, while self-catering cottages abound. Cafés like Ye Olde Naked Man and The Little House Café serve wholesome meals and top-tier teas. Malham's lodging is more limited but very atmospheric—try Beck Hall for a stream-side inn with local dishes and gardens, or the youth hostel for budget-friendly dorms in a stone manor. Vegetarian and vegan options are increasingly available across both towns, and several establishments focus on organic, seasonal produce sourced from nearby farms.

Conclusion:
Settle and Malham represent the southern Dales at their most sculptural and storied. Settle draws you in with its community energy and heritage heart; Malham pulls you outward into landscape so ancient and awe-inspiring it reshapes your sense of scale. Whether you're navigating a local footpath, exploring a fossil-strewn gorge, or sipping a fair-trade coffee while trains rumble through the valley below, the southern Dales offer a grounded, spacious kind of beauty—one that balances natural spectacle with human warmth and welcome.

6.5 Village Walks, Markets & Craft Traditions

The pace of life in the Yorkshire Dales slows the moment you step into one of its villages. You hear it in the quiet crunch of your boots on gravel paths, feel it in the easy chatter of stallholders on market day, and see it in the way old stone cottages lean gently toward one another. These villages aren't made to be rushed through. They're made to be wandered, lingered in, and remembered — one slow step, one warm conversation, one handmade item at a time.

Wandering Where the Heart Wants to Go
 Walking through a Dales village feels like wandering through a storybook. You don't need a trail map to guide you — just follow your feet. Maybe it's a narrow lane that disappears between hedgerows or a quiet path over a stiled wall leading to a stream. Birds sing overhead. Sheep rustle in the fields. You'll pass gardens blooming with foxgloves, cottages with low doors and hanging teapots, and maybe a bench where someone nods a friendly "mornin'." From Bainbridge to Burnsall, and Giggleswick to

Gunnerside, these are places best explored slowly, with a pocketful of time and no real plan.

Old Markets that Still Matter
Markets here aren't busy, shouty affairs. They're gatherings — friendly, familiar, and woven into village life. On certain days, the town square might be lined with striped awnings and wooden tables stacked with crusty loaves, woollen socks, hand-thrown mugs, and jars of bright plum jam. Folks chat under the soft drizzle or warm sun, depending on the mood of the weather. The farmers know the bakers. The weavers know the cheesemakers. And visitors, if they slow down enough, feel like they've stepped into something old and ongoing. Grassington hosts one of the most beloved market days, where the cobbled square hums with locals and visitors trading stories over bags of fudge or baskets of rhubarb.

Hands that Still Make Things From Scratch
The craft traditions in the Dales are quiet but full of soul. This isn't souvenir-shop stuff. Its pottery turned slowly on old wheels, wool spun from local sheep, candles scented with heather, and soap made with oatmilk and honey. In tucked-away barns or sunny garden studios, you'll find artists still working the old ways. Places like Farfield Mill near Sedbergh or Yore Mill in Aysgarth house whole communities of makers — weavers, printmakers, leatherworkers — who welcome you in like an old friend. They might let you try your hand at something, or simply show you what they're working on, all while the kettle's boiling in the corner.

Description:
This part of the Dales is less about destinations and more about experiences. Village life is woven with human touch — things made, grown, sold, or shown with care. Whether it's watching someone hand-bind a notebook or buying a wool throw that still smells faintly of lanolin, it's all real, grounded, and heartwarming. The walks between these villages — sometimes just a mile or two apart — are gentle and lovely. You might start the morning in a place like Litton or Austwick and end up in another hamlet by afternoon, having passed meadows, dry-stone walls, a bubbling beck, and maybe a tea break under an old oak.

Location:
Found throughout the National Park but especially rich in the southern Dales (around Settle, Malham, Austwick), Upper Wensleydale (near Bainbridge, Askrigg, and Hawes), Wharfedale (Grassington, Burnsall, Hebden), and Swaledale (Reeth, Muker, Gunnerside). Market days vary by village — for example, Grassington hosts markets monthly, while Settle and Hawes have regular weekly ones.

Key Features:
Gentle village-to-village walks, local craft studios, regular traditional markets, warm community feel, slow and scenic routes, authentic food and goods, opportunities to meet real craftspeople.

Visitor Services:
Public toilets in most villages (usually near the car parks), cafes and tearooms for rest stops, helpful visitor centers in larger hubs like Hawes and Grassington, community noticeboards with events and walk suggestions, village shops for essentials, and seasonal bus routes between towns for easy returns if walking one-way.

Price:
Walks are free and open to all. Markets are free to attend, with food or crafts ranging from $3 to $50 depending on item. Handmade wool goods and art pieces may range higher. Studios may offer workshops from around $20 to $60 per session.

Contact Address:
For Grassington Market: Grassington Hub, 2 Garrs Ln, Grassington, Skipton BD23 5AT.
For Farfield Mill: Garsdale Rd, Sedbergh LA10 5LW.
Yore Mill Craft Shop & Gallery: Aysgarth Falls, Leyburn DL8 3SR.

Website:
Grassington Hub: www.grassingtonhub.com
Farfield Mill: www.farfieldmill.org
Yore Mill: www.yoremillcraftshop.co.uk

Conclusion:
The soul of the Dales lives not just in the hills, but in its villages — in the rhythm of the walks, the hum of markets, and the stories behind every handmade thing. Come not to buy, but to connect. Let your feet wander, your heart slow, and your hands reach for something real.

Chapter 7: Historic Sites & Cultural Heritage

7.1 Bolton Abbey & the River Wharfe

The moment you pass through the stone gate and set foot on the soft grass at Bolton Abbey, time starts to stretch. Everything quiets. You hear the ripple of the River Wharfe, gentle as a whisper, and the slow rustle of leaves overhead. The ruins of the 12th-century priory rise ahead, noble and broken, as if they've been waiting for you. There's something sacred here — not just in the ancient stones, but in the stillness, the way the morning mist clings to the meadows, and the echo of every footstep along the riverbank. It feels like walking into an old story, one you somehow already know.

A Place Where Time Slows Down
Founded in 1154 by Augustinian monks, Bolton Abbey was once a thriving religious community. Though the Reformation ended its official life in the 16th century, the bones of the priory remain — arches, windows, and walls that still hold their shape against the sky. Right beside the ruins stands the Priory Church of St Mary and St Cuthbert, which is still in use today. Sunday services drift out into the grounds, blending with the sounds of birdsong and flowing water.

What makes Bolton Abbey special isn't just the history — it's how alive it all still feels. Families picnic in the shade of old trees. Dogs chase sticks into the shallows. Artists perch on camp stools with sketchbooks in their laps. Everything about the place invites you to linger. There's no rush, no agenda — just space to breathe, walk, and let the land speak.

Crossing the Stepping Stones
There are two bridges across the River Wharfe here, but the real joy lies in crossing the 60 old stepping stones just below the priory. Kids take them with arms stretched wide, giggling with each careful step. Grownups do too, some barefoot, holding their shoes in one hand. If the water's high or your balance feels uncertain, the footbridge beside the stones offers an easier crossing. But there's something childlike and thrilling in taking the old path, stone by stone, across the shining water.

Wandering the Valley of Light and Green
Bolton Abbey's estate stretches for miles — over 30,000 acres of moor, woodland, meadow, and riverbank. There are more than 80 miles of footpaths here, each one leading somewhere worth discovering. The riverside walk to the Strid is a favourite. It begins gently along level paths beneath broad trees and then narrows, climbing slightly as the water speeds up. The Strid itself is a narrow, roaring channel where the Wharfe suddenly compresses between tight rock walls. It's beautiful — and dangerous. Locals will tell you tales of its hidden power, how people and even animals have disappeared beneath the surface. You don't swim here. You watch and wonder.

Other walks lead up through fields of wildflowers, past sheep grazing near stone barns, through quiet woods filled with the smell of damp earth and moss. Spring brings bluebells and birdsong; autumn brings gold light and rustling leaves. You can take short, family-friendly strolls or spend a whole day walking and never feel you've seen the same place twice.

Local Food, Firesides & Tearoom Comforts
After hours outdoors, there's nothing better than something warm and homemade. Luckily, Bolton Abbey's estate has you covered. The Cavendish Pavilion, down by the river, feels like a mix between a country café and a Victorian lodge. It's glassy and bright,

with views across the river and a menu full of local favourites — thick soups, buttered scones, hearty pies, and plenty of Yorkshire tea. There's also the Tea Cottage near the priory, smaller and simpler, but just as welcoming, with outdoor seating in good weather and the smell of fresh baking drawing you in.

For a proper sit-down meal, head to the nearby village of Bolton Abbey (same name, different place) where The Devonshire Arms Hotel & Spa offers elegant dining with local produce, or cozy pub classics by the fire at The Tea on the Green. Whether you're after a picnic sandwich or a celebratory lunch, you'll eat well here — and locally.

Location:
Bolton Abbey Estate, Skipton BD23 6EX, North Yorkshire, England

Key Features:

- 12th-century priory ruins and functioning church
- 80+ miles of walking paths
- Stepping stones and scenic river views
- Estate grounds with ancient woodland and moor
- Family-friendly facilities and trails
- Accessible walking routes and bridges
- Wildlife and seasonal flowers

Visitor Services:

- On-site cafés and tearooms
- Picnic areas
- Pay & display car parks at several entrances (Riverside, Strid Wood, Barden Tower)
- Public toilets with baby-changing facilities
- Estate gift shops and visitor centres
- Guided walks and educational signs
- Dog-friendly areas (dogs must be on leads near livestock and in specific zones)

Price:
Entry to the estate is free for walkers. Car parking is the main charge:

- £15 per car per day (high season)
- £12 in off-peak times
- Annual passes available for regular visitors

Contact Address:
Bolton Abbey Estate Office

Bolton Abbey
Skipton
North Yorkshire
BD23 6EX
Phone: +44 (0)1756 718000
Email: estate@boltonabbey.com

Website:
https://www.boltonabbey.com

Pro tip:
Come early in the day or later in the afternoon to avoid the busiest times. Weekday mornings, especially out of school holidays, offer a rare peace — when it's just you, the river, and the wind moving through the trees.

For your safety and theirs:
The River Wharfe can change quickly with rainfall. Always keep children close near the water and don't attempt to cross the stepping stones in high flow. The Strid, while beautiful, is extremely dangerous — stay well back from the edge.

Conclusion:
Bolton Abbey is more than a historic site — it's a full experience of place, memory, and natural beauty. Whether you come for a quick stroll or a full day of wandering, you'll leave with more than you expected. The peace stays with you, tucked somewhere deep, like a small gift from the Dales.

7.2 Jervaulx Abbey & Hidden Monastic Ruins

The ruins of Jervaulx Abbey rise gently out of a wildflower meadow, half-swallowed by ivy, surrounded by silence and sky. Unlike more curated English Heritage sites, Jervaulx is beautifully raw — open, unguarded, and still touched by mystery. There are no ticket lines, no polished visitor centres. Just a discreet honesty box at the gate and a quiet sense that something sacred once happened here. A wander through these ruins feels intimate, even haunting. The walls don't shout history — they whisper it.

A Monastery Lost to Time and Ivy

Jervaulx Abbey was founded in 1156 by the Cistercian order, originally a daughter house of Byland Abbey. The monks settled beside the River Ure, seeking isolation, simplicity, and a life of prayer and self-sufficiency. What they built here flourished — not just in spiritual power but in agricultural wealth. Jervaulx became one of the wealthiest Cistercian monasteries in the north of England, known especially for its sheep pastures, skilled book production, and early cheese-making that laid the groundwork for today's Wensleydale traditions.

All of it came to a quiet halt in 1537 during Henry VIII's brutal Dissolution of the Monasteries. The abbey was stripped, its lands sold off, and its brothers scattered. Over the centuries, the ruins became overgrown and almost forgotten. And yet, that's part of what makes them powerful. This isn't a place of grand tourist spectacles. It's a place you stumble upon — and feel.

Walking Through Ghosts and Greenery
Today, Jervaulx is privately owned and maintained by the Burdon family, who've kept it accessible while protecting its unspoiled spirit. As you step into the grounds, you won't find manicured lawns or interpretive displays. Instead, you walk through high grasses and low arches. The abbey's remains — church nave, chapter house, cloisters, infirmary — are scattered like fallen thoughts across the field. Wildflowers bloom in the cracks of weathered stone. Birds nest in what were once dormitories.

This freedom of access makes Jervaulx unforgettable. Children can run between pillars. Artists sketch in quiet corners. Couples bring picnics and sit with backs against warm walls. There are no barriers or roped-off zones. The place invites intimacy. You can put your hand on the cold limestone and feel the weight of centuries.

A Living Landscape of Monastic Memory
One of the most evocative features of Jervaulx is how its ruin has become part of the landscape. Vines drape over archways. The grass underfoot is soft and uneven. In spring and summer, bees hum through thick banks of foxglove and wild thyme. Butterflies flicker through broken windows. You feel like the monastery never fully disappeared — it just shifted form, becoming part of the natural order it once tried to control.

Unlike better-known ruins like Rievaulx or Fountains, Jervaulx feels like a secret. There are days when you might have it entirely to yourself. No tour buses. No gift shops. Just the sound of the wind and the distant murmur of the River Ure. In a world of constant stimulation, this quiet — this soft crumbling into beauty — is its own kind of treasure.

Tearooms, Cheese & the Spirit of Simplicity
Just across from the abbey gates lies the family-run Jervaulx Tearooms — a beloved local stop known for hearty soups, fresh-baked cakes, and thick-cut sandwiches. It's the sort of place where walkers kick off muddy boots and linger over pots of Yorkshire tea. In summer, the garden seating buzzes with bees and conversation. In cooler months, the inside is cozy and simple, with the warm smell of baking and slow-cooked stews.

The tearoom sources much of its produce locally and offers vegetarian and gluten-free options. It's also the best nearby place to sample Wensleydale cheese — a nod to the monastic past. Whether you stop for lunch or just a sweet treat after your walk through the abbey, the atmosphere feels perfectly in tune with the site: calm, nourishing, unpretentious.

Nearby Wanderings Along the Ure

From Jervaulx, it's easy to extend your exploration. Walking paths connect the abbey with the nearby River Ure and the surrounding pastureland. A popular and peaceful trail leads downstream towards Cover Bridge and the village of East Witton, offering views of rolling fields, dry-stone walls, and grazing sheep. This stretch of the Ure Valley feels timeless. Bring binoculars if you're a birdwatcher — herons, kingfishers, and even red kites are often spotted here.

Jervaulx Park, the surrounding estate, also holds remnants of old medieval fish ponds, stone walls, and woodland groves once cultivated by the monks. You can follow footpaths that trace the edges of this hidden past, with just enough signage to orient but not overwhelm.

Location:
Jervaulx Abbey, Park House, Jervaulx, Ripon, North Yorkshire HG4 4PH, England

Key Features:

- 12th-century Cistercian abbey ruins
- Peaceful, natural setting with wildflowers and open access
- No barriers or tourist infrastructure — immersive experience
- Family-run tearooms across the road
- Close to River Ure walking paths and scenic valley views
- Heritage linked to origins of Wensleydale cheese

Visitor Services:

- Free open access year-round (donation via honesty box encouraged)
- On-site tearooms with indoor and outdoor seating
- Small parking area available near the tearoom
- Dog-friendly (dogs must be on leads due to livestock)
- No public toilets on-site; facilities available at the tearooms
- No official guides or maps — self-led experience
- Cash and card accepted at the tearooms

Price:

There is no formal entrance fee. Visitors are kindly asked to leave a donation in the honesty box at the gate. Suggested donation:

- Adults: £4

- Children: £2
- Families: £10

Contact Address:
Jervaulx Abbey
Park House
Jervaulx
Ripon
North Yorkshire
HG4 4PH
Phone: +44 (0)1677 460391
Email: info@jervaulxabbey.com

Website:
https://www.jervaulxabbey.com

Pro tip:
Visit just after sunrise or in late evening light. The abbey takes on a golden glow, and you're more likely to have the place to yourself. In autumn, the surrounding trees turn copper and amber — it's like stepping into a living painting.

Bring the following essentials:

- Walking shoes suitable for uneven ground
- Picnic blanket if you plan to stay longer
- Cash for donations or the tearoom (card accepted, but cash still preferred)
- Binoculars for birdwatching
- A camera — the light here changes everything

For your safety and theirs:
Though the ruins are open, tread carefully — the ground is uneven, and the stones can be slippery when wet. Children should be supervised, and climbing on the walls is strongly discouraged.

Conclusion:
Jervaulx Abbey doesn't dazzle with grandeur — it speaks with quiet grace. In its softened edges, wildflowers, and wind-worn walls, it offers something rare: a spiritual hush, a deep-rooted beauty that doesn't need explanation. It's a place to sit still, to remember that history doesn't always live in museums — sometimes, it waits in the grass, blooming gently between the stones.

7.3 Castles, Towers & Ancient Trails

Across the Yorkshire Dales, castle ruins crown hilltops, tower houses sit nestled in secluded valleys, and ancient tracks wind between moors and meadows. These aren't just relics of war and power — they are guardians of the past, standing quietly in landscapes shaped by centuries. From Norman strongholds to medieval hunting lodges, each castle or tower tells a story of kings, monks, rebels, and shepherds. And it's not just the buildings that hold intrigue — the trails connecting them are equally rich with legend and life. In this region, a walk isn't just a walk; it's a journey across time.

Description:
The castles and towers of the Dales were often built less for glamour and more for defense, administration, or symbolism. Unlike the royal castles of southern England,

many here are smaller, sturdier, and built from local limestone. Some are crumbling into ruin, while others have been carefully restored. But all are rooted in the land — part of the landscape rather than dominating it.

Among the most notable is **Bolton Castle**, a striking and remarkably complete medieval fortress in Wensleydale. Further east lies **Middleham Castle**, the childhood home of Richard III. Across the valleys are smaller but no less fascinating tower houses, such as **Nappa Hall** near Askrigg or the remote **Pendragon Castle** in Mallerstang. And connecting these strongholds are old routes once walked by soldiers, pilgrims, traders, and farmers — trails like the **Cam High Road**, the **Roman Road above Malham**, and the **Lady Anne's Way**.

Location:
The castles, towers, and trails described here are scattered across the Yorkshire Dales National Park, primarily in the regions of Wensleydale, Swaledale, and the southern Dales.

Key Features:

- Authentic, mostly unrestored medieval ruins
- Restored strongholds with interpretation centres
- Waymarked ancient trails and Roman roads
- Hidden towers in lesser-visited valleys
- Opportunities for long walks, circular hikes, and family-friendly exploration
- Deep ties to key historical figures like Richard III and Lady Anne Clifford

Visitor Services:
Depending on the site, services may include on-site cafés, interpretation boards, gift shops, guided tours, and walking maps. Remote ruins such as Pendragon Castle have no facilities, so preparation is essential. Larger sites like Bolton and Middleham offer full visitor services, toilets, and nearby eateries.

Price:

- Bolton Castle: Adults £12.50, Children £6.50, Family tickets from £34
- Middleham Castle (managed by English Heritage): Adults £8.10, Children £4.90
- Nappa Hall: No public access (view from public footpath only)
- Pendragon Castle: Free (open access)
- Trails: Free to walk (parking fees may apply at start points)

Contact Address:
Bolton Castle
Castle Bolton

Leyburn
North Yorkshire
DL8 4ET
Phone: +44 (0)1969 623981
Website: www.boltoncastle.co.uk

Middleham Castle (English Heritage)
Castle Hill
Middleham
Leyburn
North Yorkshire
DL8 4QG
Phone: +44 (0)1969 623899
Website: www.english-heritage.org.uk

Bolton Castle:
One of the best-preserved medieval castles in England, Bolton was built in the late 14th century by Richard le Scrope, Lord Chancellor to Richard II. It once held Mary, Queen of Scots, as a royal prisoner for six months — her chamber and the privy she used can still be seen. The castle's layout is square, with four towers, and much of the structure remains intact. There's a recreated medieval garden, a small falconry, and costumed events in summer. Children enjoy the atmospheric dungeon and the narrow stone staircases. The views over Wensleydale are unforgettable, especially when mist hangs low in the morning.

Middleham Castle:
Just a short drive (or a lovely walk) from Bolton, Middleham Castle was once known as the "Windsor of the North." This was Richard III's childhood home and base of power when he was Duke of Gloucester. The castle itself is imposing — a massive stone kept surrounded by curtain walls — though much of it is ruinous. English Heritage maintains the site, with interpretation boards and models. The small shop sells local history books, and the grounds are ideal for a sunny picnic. Middleham village itself is charming, with tea shops and a quiet square, making it a great base for history buffs.

Pendragon Castle:
Deep in the remote Mallerstang Valley, Pendragon is as romantic as ruins come. Said to have been founded by Uther Pendragon, the mythical father of King Arthur (though no evidence supports this), the castle's real history is 12th-century Norman. It was once held by the powerful Clifford family, and was rebuilt several times before being abandoned in the 17th century. Now, it's a roofless shell with crumbling turrets and mossy walls, but the setting is pure magic: hills rolling all around, the River Eden

bubbling nearby, and barely another soul in sight. There's no entrance fee, no visitor centre — just you and the echoes of time.

Nappa Hall:
This private manor near Askrigg was originally built as a fortified house in the 15th century. Though not open to the public, it's worth passing by on the walking route from Askrigg to Bainbridge, as the exterior remains striking. It's an excellent example of a Yorkshire tower house, with battlements and arrow slits visible from the footpath.

Ancient Trails to Walk:
Lady Anne's Way traces the route of Lady Anne Clifford, a 17th-century noblewoman who restored many castles and churches across the north. Her legacy lives on in the stonework and style-markers along this 100-mile walk from Skipton to Penrith. It passes both Pendragon and Brougham Castles.

The **Cam High Road** is a Roman track that leads from Bainbridge across the moors toward Ingleton. It offers expansive views and a clear sense of walking in the footsteps of centuries. Another evocative path is the **Monk's Road**, leading between Nidderdale and Wharfedale, once used by monastic communities.

The **Malham Roman Road** curves up from the village toward Mastiles Lane, once a Roman marching route and later a monastic drive road. Today it's popular with walkers for its views, solitude, and signs of old cobbled surfaces underfoot.

Pro tip:
Download or pick up OS Explorer maps before setting out. Some castle sites like Pendragon are remote with no signage, so map-reading skills are useful. If you're interested in combining multiple sites into a multi-day trek, consider basing yourself in Leyburn or Hawes, both well connected to trails and public transport.

Bring the following essentials:

- Good hiking boots (paths around Pendragon and Cam High Road are often boggy)
- Waterproof layers
- Binoculars (great birdlife along the trails)
- Packed lunch and water bottle (remote sites have no services)
- A camera with wide-angle lens for landscapes and ruins

For your safety and theirs:
Most castle ruins are unfenced and uneven. Be cautious of loose stone, steep stairs, and unstable walls. Dogs are welcome on leads. Always follow Countryside Code guidelines — close gates, don't disturb livestock, and leave no trace.

Conclusion:

The castles and towers of the Dales are more than monuments — they are living punctuation marks in the story of this land. Whether you're gazing out from the battlements of Bolton or tracing Lady Anne's determined footsteps across the moors, these places offer more than history. They offer connections. To landscape. To legend. And to a deeper sense of time than most modern travels can provide.

7.4 Museums, Heritage Centres & Storytelling

The Yorkshire Dales are not just shaped by rivers and ridges — they are shaped by people. Farmers, miners, monks, shepherds, artisans, and everyday villagers have left behind not just dry facts, but rich stories that still echo through barns, chapels, mills, and market halls. Across the region, museums and heritage centres bring these voices to life. They are not grand national institutions but small, deeply rooted spaces run by local communities, historians, and volunteers who care deeply about their place in the world. Here, storytelling isn't a luxury — it's a living, breathing act of preservation.

Description:

The museums of the Yorkshire Dales are uniquely grounded. Rather than sterile halls of dusty exhibits, they tend to occupy old buildings: railway stations, chapels, mills, workhouses, or townhouses that once belonged to tradespeople. Exhibits are tactile and personal — shepherd's crooks, butter churns, pit lamps, and children's toys used by real people from the surrounding hills and villages. Beyond static displays, many centres offer films, walking tours, hands-on crafts, or seasonal storytelling events.

Whether you're interested in lead mining or Quaker settlements, rural childhoods or Victorian railways, you'll find a space that celebrates it with pride and intimacy. In particular, places like the **Dales Countryside Museum, Swaledale Museum, Skipton's Craven Museum**, and **The Folly in Settle** stand out for their authentic storytelling and depth.

Location:
These museums and heritage centres are spread throughout the Yorkshire Dales National Park and its surrounding towns. Key sites are located in Hawes, Reeth, Skipton, Settle, Grassington, Dent, and Richmond.

Key Features:

- Authentic local artefacts from farming, mining, and village life
- Community-curated exhibitions with rotating themes
- Historical buildings with immersive interpretation
- Storytelling events, talks, and local walking tours
- Interactive exhibits for children and families
- Quiet, reflective spaces ideal for slow travel

Visitor Services:
Facilities typically include welcome desks, small gift shops, on-site or nearby cafés, toilets, and accessibility adaptations. Most museums are wheelchair-accessible and offer printed guides or audio tours. Heritage centres in remote villages may have limited opening days, so checking ahead is advised.

Price:

- Dales Countryside Museum: Adults £5.50, Children £3.00, Family tickets from £13.50
- Swaledale Museum: £4.00 suggested donation
- Craven Museum (Skipton): Free admission
- The Folly (Settle): Adults £5.00, Children free
- Dent Village Heritage Centre: Adults £4.50, Children £2.50

Contact Address:
Dales Countryside Museum
Station Yard
Hawes

North Yorkshire
DL8 3NT
Phone: +44 (0)1969 666210
Website: www.yorkshiredales.org.uk

Swaledale Museum
The Green
Reeth
Richmond
North Yorkshire
DL11 6TX
Phone: +44 (0)1748 884118
Website: www.swaledalemuseum.org

Dales Countryside Museum, Hawes:
Housed in the old Hawes railway station, this museum is the flagship interpretive centre of the Yorkshire Dales National Park Authority. It tells the layered story of life in the Dales, from prehistoric settlements to modern sheep farming. Highlights include a recreated Victorian kitchen, a lead mining tunnel exhibit, and a hand-knitting room with interactive looms. Outside, the preserved steam engine and railway platform conjure images of the old Wensleydale railway line, still partially in use today. Seasonal exhibitions delve into current themes — from sustainable farming to hilltop folklore — and there's a lovely café right next door.

Swaledale Museum, Reeth:
Small but packed with heart, this volunteer-run gem focuses on the life, work, and language of upper Swaledale. Its stone-walled rooms are lined with lead mining tools, butter paddles, and homemade furniture from isolated farmsteads. There's also a beautiful textile collection that includes handwoven Swaledale wool garments and Quaker bonnets. What makes it especially rewarding is the personal curation — every item is labeled with context and, often, a story. Talks, guided walks, and evening storytelling sessions take place in summer. Entry is by donation, and the experience is intimate and heartfelt.

Craven Museum, Skipton:
Located inside Skipton Town Hall, the Craven Museum is a thoroughly modernised space that still honors its Victorian roots. Interactive exhibits explore the region's geology, archaeology, textile industries, and local writers, including the famous playwright JB Priestley. The standout feature is a rare copy of Shakespeare's First Folio on display — a quiet treasure in a modest space. Children enjoy the 'Time Explorers' interactive games, and the attached concert hall often hosts folk music and literary

events. Being free to enter, it's a great stop for families or travellers wanting to better understand the area's cultural bedrock.

The Folly, Settle:
A striking 17th-century townhouse now turned heritage centre, The Folly explores the story of Settle and the wider Craven area. Its architecture alone is worth a visit, with massive stone fireplaces, oak beams, and mullioned windows. Inside, exhibits range from the Settle-Carlisle Railway to the rise and fall of local wool merchants. The museum's storytelling approach is immersive — using audio stations, film, and diary excerpts from real townspeople across centuries. Special exhibitions often focus on contemporary interpretations of rural identity, and the café is a quiet place to reflect with a local herbal tea.

Dent Village Heritage Centre:
Nestled in the sleepy village of Dent, this centre offers a compelling look at life in the Western Dales. Exhibits include the story of Adam Sedgwick — a Dent-born pioneer of modern geology — and the rise of 'terrible knitters,' whose fine gloves and stockings once supported the valley economy. The railway room tells of the engineering marvels of the Settle-Carlisle line, while the farmstead room showcases rare tools, spinning wheels, and sheep breeds like the Swaledale and Herdwick. There's also a tearoom and shop selling handmade crafts and books.

Pro tip:
Combine museum visits with village walks. For example, after exploring the Dales Countryside Museum in Hawes, follow the footpath to Hardraw Force or loop around to Gayle Mill. In Settle, pair The Folly with a walk up Castleberg Crag for sweeping views and a picnic.

Bring the following essentials:

- Notebook or journal for reflections (many museums invite you to share your own memories)
- A good map if planning village-to-village routes
- Cash for small entry fees and donations
- Time to linger — these aren't 'checklist' museums, but slow, soul-fed experiences

For your safety and theirs:
Some centres are housed in old buildings with narrow staircases or low ceilings. Wear supportive shoes and take care when navigating uneven floors. Most sites are well maintained, but it's best to confirm accessibility needs in advance.

Conclusion:
The museums and heritage centres of the Yorkshire Dales do far more than preserve

artefacts — they preserve the spirit of a people and place. Through lovingly kept ledgers, hand-stitched smocks, and tales told aloud on summer evenings, they invite you not just to observe history, but to feel it. In these modest buildings scattered through valleys and market towns, the past is still alive — and you're warmly invited in to listen.

Chapter 8: Outdoor Activities & Exploration

8.1 Circular Walks & Short Hikes

The Yorkshire Dales isn't just a place to admire from the roadside — it's a place best experienced on foot. Circular walks and short hikes offer a perfect balance for those who want to deeply immerse themselves in nature without committing to strenuous day-long treks. From gentle riverside strolls to rugged moorland loops, the Dales offers countless well-marked circular routes that bring you back to your starting point, ideal for visitors using local villages as base camps. Whether you're visiting with children, seniors, or simply seeking meditative solitude, these short and scenic circuits provide the essence of Dales walking — unhurried, breathtaking, and soulful.

Description:

Short circular walks in the Dales often lead you through atmospheric limestone pavements, hidden waterfalls, old packhorse bridges, sheep-studded meadows, and historic hamlets. Most are between 2 and 6 miles in length and can be completed in 1 to 3 hours, with plenty of time for resting, picnicking, and exploring. Waymarked signs and local walking maps ensure you can follow the paths confidently, and the routes usually start and end in a village with a tea room or heritage site, giving each walk a rewarding sense of completion.

These hikes are particularly special because they are deeply woven into the fabric of local life. Many routes follow ancient tracks once used by drovers or monks, with dry-stone walls guiding your steps. The Dales Way, the Ribble Way, and the Pennine Way all intersect or inspire these smaller loops, and each one offers its own unique snapshot of Dale's life — seasonal lambing, springtime wildflowers, autumn fog rolling off the hills, or the crystalline stillness of a winter morning.

Location:

Circular walks are available across the national park. Popular regions include Wharfedale (Grassington, Burnsall), Swaledale (Reeth, Muker), Malhamdale (Malham, Kirkby Malham), Wensleydale (Aysgarth, Hawes), and Ribblesdale (Settle, Stainforth). Many routes begin from local car parks, bus stops, or information centres.

Key Features:

- Walks range from 2 to 6 miles (1.5 to 3 hours average)
- Routes are waymarked or easy to follow with an OS map
- Terrain includes riverside paths, woodlands, pastureland, and upland moors
- Many routes pass heritage sites, waterfalls, or traditional farms
- Perfect for casual walkers, families, photographers, and nature lovers

Visitor Services:

Most starting points offer public parking, toilets, benches, and nearby cafés or pubs. Visitor centres in Malham, Reeth, Hawes, and Grassington provide walking leaflets, maps, and local tips. Some areas have downloadable audio trails or QR codes for digital interpretation. Mobile signals can be limited, so it's recommended to carry a physical map.

Price:

All walks are free of charge. Parking may range from £2 to £5 at local car parks. Donations to local maintenance trusts or honesty boxes help preserve paths and signage.

Pro tip:

Always check the weather before you go and dress accordingly — waterproof boots, layers, and a windproof jacket are essential. In spring and summer, bring insect repellent and sun protection. A flask of tea and a Yorkshire curd tart from a local bakery can make your mid-walk rest even more memorable.

Top Recommended Circular Walks:

Malham Cove Circular (Approx. 4.5 miles):
A classic loop starting in the village of Malham, this walk leads you through some of the Dales' most dramatic limestone scenery. You'll climb up to the breathtaking Malham Cove, pass through the narrow gorge of Gordale Scar, and optionally detour to Janet's Foss waterfall. The route is moderately strenuous with a well-maintained stone staircase and sweeping views. Perfect for geology lovers and landscape photographers.

Location: Start and finish at Malham National Park Centre, BD23 4DA

Grassington to Hebden Loop (Approx. 3 miles):
This gentle riverside loop follows the River Wharfe from the cobbled streets of Grassington to the smaller village of Hebden and back. You'll pass through wildflower meadows and spot old mining remnants along Hebden Beck. Especially lovely in spring and early summer, this walk is easy to moderate, suitable for all ages.

Location: Start at Grassington car park, BD23 5LB

Reeth & Fremington Edge Circular (Approx. 5 miles):
This loop climbs steadily from Reeth to Fremington Edge, offering panoramic views over Swaledale before descending through meadows and sheep pastures. The path is a little steeper in places, so walking poles may be helpful. Best enjoyed in the late afternoon light for golden valley views.

Location: Start in Reeth village green, DL11 6TX

Aysgarth Falls Circular (Approx. 2.5 miles):
Combining riverside ease with woodland beauty, this short loop visits the Upper, Middle, and Lower Falls of the River Ure at Aysgarth. There are picnic benches, well-placed viewing platforms, and a tea room at the visitor centre. A gentle, family-friendly walk that's especially powerful after rainfall.

Location: Start at Aysgarth Falls National Park Centre, DL8 3TH

Ingleton Waterfalls Trail (Approx. 4 miles):
Privately maintained but open to the public for a fee, this circular walk takes you through a dramatic landscape of waterfalls, woodlands, and limestone cliffs. While more commercial and popular than other routes, it offers a theatrical experience of the Dales' water-carved terrain.

Price: Adults £8, Children £4
Location: Start at Broadwood Entrance, Ingleton, LA6 3ET
Website: www.ingletonwaterfallstrail.co.uk

Stainforth & Catrigg Force Loop (Approx. 3 miles):

Starting from the historic packhorse bridge in Stainforth, this moderate hike leads through pastures and woodland to the secluded Catrigg Force waterfall, hidden in a fern-filled glen. The descent offers striking views of Pen-y-ghent on clear days.

Location: Start at Stainforth car park, BD24 9PF

Before your trip:

- Download or purchase an OS Explorer Map (OL2, OL30, OL19 cover most of the Dales)
- Check parking availability and toilet facilities at your starting point
- Pack light, but bring water, snacks, a rainproof jacket, and a charged phone
- If walking solo, leave your route plan with someone

Bring the following essentials:

- Comfortable, waterproof walking shoes or boots
- Layered clothing and a small daypack
- Local trail map or downloaded route
- Water bottle and snacks
- First aid kit and walking pole (optional)
- Phone with offline maps or GPS

For your safety and theirs:

Stick to marked paths and close gates behind you. Do not disturb livestock or climb over dry-stone walls. Take all litter home and avoid picking wildflowers. In foggy or wet weather, avoid exposed ridges or steep descents. Dogs should be kept on leads, especially during lambing season.

Conclusion:

Short circular walks in the Yorkshire Dales are more than just easy exercise — they're soulful journeys into the land's natural rhythms and human past. Each footstep connects you with centuries of quiet passage — monks, shepherds, mill workers, and now, you. Whether walking in the hush of a drystone corridor or pausing by a stone bridge over rushing water, these gentle loops remind you that sometimes, the most profound travel requires only your feet and a willingness to wander.

8.2 Long-Distance Trails: Pennine Way & Dales Way

The Yorkshire Dales form the dramatic heartland of two of Britain's most iconic long-distance footpaths: the Pennine Way and the Dales Way. These trails aren't simply about covering distance — they are pilgrimages into the soul of the northern landscape. Winding through remote moorlands, ancient villages, limestone cliffs, and flower-filled dales, both routes offer walkers an unparalleled opportunity to connect with the rhythms of nature, history, and solitude. Whether you undertake the full length of these trails or walk just a stretch, they leave a deep imprint — one shaped by wild winds, kindness from strangers, and the comforting crunch of boots on old stone.

Description:

The **Pennine Way** is often referred to as Britain's first National Trail and its most challenging. Running for 268 miles from Edale in Derbyshire to Kirk Yetholm in the Scottish Borders, the trail cuts directly through the Yorkshire Dales for about 80 miles. This central section includes some of the most dramatic and character-defining terrain: high moorland plateaus, hauntingly quiet valleys, peat bogs, and iconic climbs like Pen-y-ghent and Malham Cove. It's suited to experienced hikers who are well-prepared for long days in sometimes remote and wild conditions.

The **Dales Way**, by contrast, offers a gentler and more pastoral experience. Stretching 80 miles from Ilkley in West Yorkshire to Bowness-on-Windermere in the Lake District, it follows riverside paths and valley floors for much of its journey. This trail offers sweeping views of hills without often climbing them, making it a favourite for walkers of all ages and abilities. The Yorkshire Dales section of the Dales Way is considered its most scenic, winding past abbeys, packhorse bridges, meadows, and charming villages like Buckden and Dent.

Both routes are typically walked from south to north and can be completed over the course of a week or more. Many hikers opt to walk these trails in segments over months or years, using public transport or local inns as base points. The local footpath network often connects to both trails, allowing for circular day hikes or diversions to notable landmarks, cafés, or hidden waterfalls.

Location:

The **Pennine Way** enters the Yorkshire Dales near Cowling and continues north through Malham, Horton-in-Ribblesdale, Pen-y-ghent, Hawes, and Hardraw before leaving the park beyond Tan Hill Inn.
The **Dales Way** begins in Ilkley and crosses into the Dales via Bolton Abbey, Burnsall, Grassington, Kettlewell, Buckden, and Dentdale before entering Cumbria en route to Bowness-on-Windermere.

Key Features:

- The Pennine Way: 268 miles total, ~80 miles in the Yorkshire Dales
- The Dales Way: 80 miles total, ~45 miles in the Yorkshire Dales
- Terrain ranges from limestone cliffs and open moorland to riverside meadows
- Highlights include Pen-y-ghent, Malham Cove, Ribblehead Viaduct, Bolton Abbey, Dentdale
- Trails intersect with heritage sites, traditional villages, and remote farmsteads
- Excellent signage and frequent guidebooks or waymarking help with navigation

Visitor Services:
Both trails offer a well-developed support system of walker-friendly inns, hostels, B&Bs, and baggage transfer services. In key villages such as Malham, Horton-in-Ribblesdale, Grassington, and Buckden, you'll find accommodation, small grocers, cafés, and pubs offering hearty, non-alcoholic meals, packed lunches, and local advice. National Park visitor centres in Grassington, Malham, and Hawes stock maps, books, and trail information. Mobile reception is generally good in valleys but limited on moorland tops. Bus and rail links at Ilkley, Settle, Garsdale, and Dent make staging your walk manageable.

Price:
Free to walk. Accommodation along the trails ranges from £35 per night in hostels to £80–£150 per night in B&Bs or guesthouses. Baggage transfer services average £8–£12 per bag, per stage. OS Explorer maps or trail guidebooks cost around £10–£15.

Pro tip:
If you're walking a section and want minimal planning, use a local company offering self-guided walking holidays — they'll book your accommodation, provide maps and GPX files, and transfer your bags. This is particularly useful on the Pennine Way, where accommodations are further apart.

Trail Highlights in the Yorkshire Dales:

Pennine Way – Malham to Horton-in-Ribblesdale (Approx. 15 miles):
A demanding but unforgettable stage that begins with the limestone amphitheatre of Malham Cove, ascends to the exposed heights of Fountains Fell, and finally climbs the steep flanks of Pen-y-ghent before descending into Horton. Walkers are rewarded with views that stretch across the Dales and beyond. Good fitness and navigation skills are essential, especially in poor weather.

Location: Start in Malham (BD23 4DA), finish in Horton-in-Ribblesdale (BD24 0HF)

Pennine Way – Hawes to Tan Hill Inn (Approx. 17 miles):
This longer stage climbs out of Wensleydale past Hardraw Force, continues through the wilds of Great Shunner Fell, and crosses the vast moorland of Stonesdale before arriving at Tan Hill Inn — Britain's highest inn. It's a remote and atmospheric walk, often done over two days with a stop in Keld or Thwaite.

Location: Start in Hawes (DL8 3QL), finish at Tan Hill Inn (DL11 6ED)

Dales Way – Burnsall to Buckden (Approx. 16 miles):
A gentle riverside walk that passes through Grassington, Kettlewell, and Starbotton, with abundant wildflowers in spring and summer. Limestone walls, small farms, and

arched stone bridges set the tone. Suitable for moderate walkers and easily divided into shorter sections.

Location: Start in Burnsall (BD23 6BP), finish in Buckden (BD23 5JA)

Dales Way – Dent to Sedbergh (Approx. 10 miles):
One of the quietest and most reflective parts of the trail, this section winds through Dentdale, past old watermills and under the towering Dent Viaduct. With gentle ascents and rural scenery, it offers a slower pace and fewer crowds.

Location: Start in Dent village (LA10 5QJ), finish in Sedbergh (LA10 5BN)

Before your trip:

- Plan your accommodation and transport well in advance, especially in summer
- Consider walking poles, especially for steep or uneven Pennine sections
- Carry an up-to-date map and compass — fog is common on higher ground
- Use the National Trails website for route planning, trail conditions, and safety tips

Bring the following essentials:

- OS Explorer OL2, OL19, and OL30 maps (or GPX files and a backup power bank)
- High-energy snacks, lunch, and plenty of water
- Weatherproof boots and layered clothing
- Hat, gloves, sunscreen, and insect repellent
- Basic first aid kit, whistle, and a waterproof map case
- Lightweight overnight gear if planning a multi-day hike

For your safety and theirs:
Always check the weather forecast before setting out and inform someone of your route. Be aware of river crossings that may flood after rain. Avoid venturing onto high ground in poor visibility unless well-equipped and experienced. Respect farmland, wildlife, and signage, and follow the Countryside Code at all times.

Conclusion:
Walking the Pennine Way or the Dales Way is about more than ticking off miles. It's about immersion — in the stillness of a misty moor, the rhythm of a stone-rimmed river, the quiet hospitality of Dales villages, and the timeless presence of the land itself. Whether you walk a mile or eighty, these trails offer not just a route, but a way of seeing the world anew — slow, deliberate, and filled with meaning.

8.3 Cycling Routes & Scenic Byways

Cycling in the Yorkshire Dales is a deeply immersive way to experience the region's dramatic geography and rural character. The quiet lanes, sweeping valleys, and muscle-burning climbs draw cyclists from across the UK and beyond, particularly since the 2014 Tour de France shone a global spotlight on the area. From gentle riverside loops to high passes like Buttertubs, the Dales offer world-class road cycling, gravel tracks, and family-friendly rides. With a mixture of steep ascents, breathtaking descents, and picture-postcard villages where tea and cake await, the region balances challenge with restorative beauty.

Description:
The Yorkshire Dales' cycling landscape can be divided into three broad categories: **scenic road routes, gravel and off-road tracks**, and **family-friendly leisure paths**. Road cyclists flock to signature climbs such as Fleet Moss, Malham Cove, and Buttertubs Pass, which combine hairpin bends with cinematic views. These are best

tackled by experienced riders with strong fitness and proper gear, but they're well worth the effort for the views alone.

For gravel bikers and mountain bikers, old drovers' roads, bridleways, and forest trails offer quieter alternatives. The Swale Trail, for instance, is a purpose-built 12-mile route through Swaledale that's ideal for families and beginners. Off-roaders can also explore Cam High Road or the Lady Anne's Way on hybrid or gravel bikes.

For those seeking a more leisurely pace, scenic byways such as the route from Grassington to Burnsall or the rail trail from Settle to Clapham provide relatively flat terrain and plentiful rest stops, ideal for picnicking or photographing dry stone walls, grazing sheep, and roadside waterfalls.

Cycle touring is also well-supported here. National Cycle Network routes such as NCN 68 (the Pennine Cycleway) and NCN 688 (the Yorkshire Dales Cycleway) crisscross the park, offering multi-day itineraries with stopovers in cyclist-friendly B&Bs, inns, or youth hostels.

Location:
The entire Yorkshire Dales National Park is suitable for cycling, but notable hotspots include Wharfedale (Grassington, Bolton Abbey), Swaledale (Reeth, Grinton), Wensleydale (Hawes, Bainbridge), and Ribblesdale (Settle, Horton-in-Ribblesdale). Each valley offers its own blend of gradients, backroads, and scenery, with most villages connected by narrow lanes and scenic climbs.

Key Features:

- Signature climbs: Buttertubs Pass, Fleet Moss, Park Rash, Malham Tarn
- Long-distance routes: Yorkshire Dales Cycleway (130 miles), Pennine Cycleway (NCN 68)
- Family routes: Swale Trail (Reeth to Keld), Settle Loop
- Mixed terrain: tarmac, gravel bridleways, drovers' tracks, forest trails
- Rider-friendly cafés, tearooms, repair shops, and water refill points
- Bike hire and e-bike rental available in towns like Settle, Grassington, and Reeth

Visitor Services:
Most larger villages have cafés or inns that cater specifically to cyclists, often with secure bike storage, water refill taps, and hearty non-alcoholic meals made from local produce. In Grassington, Settle, and Hawes, dedicated cycle shops offer repairs, gear, and route advice. Electric bike hire is increasingly available, particularly for tackling steeper gradients without strain. Baggage transfer services and cyclist-specific accommodation listings are also growing in popularity, especially along the Yorkshire

Dales Cycleway. Public toilets, picnic areas, and emergency shelter spots are marked on cycling maps and the park's digital route planners.

Price:
Cycling is free beyond equipment or rental costs. Bike hire typically costs £25–£40 per day for standard bikes and £50–£70 for e-bikes. Full-day guided tours start from £60 per person. Accommodation ranges from £35 per night (hostels or bunk barns) to £80–£120 (B&Bs or inns). Café lunches range from £6–£12.

Website:
www.cyclethedales.org.uk offers downloadable maps, elevation profiles, and route guides
www.yorkshiredales.org.uk provides National Park-endorsed trail information
www.sustrans.org.uk hosts information on NCN 68 and NCN 688

Pro tip:
Start your day early to beat the traffic and winds on high passes. Midweek riding is far quieter than weekends. Always carry cash, as rural cafés and honesty boxes may not accept cards.

Top Routes to Explore:

Yorkshire Dales Cycleway (NCN 688) – 130 Miles (210 km):
A full loop of the National Park, usually ridden over 4–7 days. It begins and ends in Skipton, travelling clockwise or counterclockwise through Grassington, Kettlewell, Hawes, Dent, and Sedbergh. The route includes both challenging climbs and sweeping descents, with plenty of scenic valleys, waterfalls, and cultural sites along the way. Ideal for experienced cyclists looking to explore the entire region.

Location: Start/finish in Skipton (BD23 1RD) – entire loop around the park

Swale Trail – 12 Miles (19 km):
Designed for families and beginners, this traffic-free route runs from Reeth to Keld, offering a mix of gentle gravel trails and country lanes. Passing through Swaledale, it follows the River Swale and offers a rewarding introduction to the Dales. With picnic stops, story boards, and wildflower meadows, it's perfect for younger riders or those new to cycling.

Location: Start in Reeth (DL11 6SZ), finish in Keld (DL11 6LJ)

Buttertubs Pass – 15 Miles Return (24 km):
This ride starts in Hawes, climbs steeply up the Buttertubs Pass, and descends into Swaledale near Thwaite. One of the most iconic cycling routes in Britain, it features in

many competitive races due to its tough gradient and exposed scenery. The climb is not long but very steep — recommended only for fit, experienced riders.

Location: Start/return in Hawes (DL8 3QL)

Settle Loop – 10 Miles (16 km):
This moderate off-road trail for mountain or hybrid bikes circles above Settle with views over Ribblesdale and the Three Peaks. Including limestone tracks, short climbs, and bridleways, it's a rewarding loop for adventure riders. Can be combined with café stops in Settle or a visit to nearby Victoria Cave.

Location: Start and finish in Settle (BD24 9EJ)

Grassington to Malham – 20 Miles Return (32 km):
A scenic lane-based route through Wharfedale and over toward Malham Tarn. It climbs steadily from Grassington via Kilnsey, then descends past Malham Cove. The return route can be looped or reversed. Suitable for road cyclists with moderate experience.

Location: Start in Grassington (BD23 5LB), turn around at Malham (BD23 4DA)

Before your trip:

- Check the weather — winds and fog can be strong on open passes
- Pack plenty of water, snacks, and layered clothing
- Carry a repair kit, spare tube, and a pump — some stretches are remote
- Download maps in advance or carry a paper version; signal can be poor
- Ensure your brakes and gears are in excellent working condition before riding steep gradients

Bring the following essentials:

- Helmet, gloves, and padded cycling shorts
- High-visibility vest or jacket and bike lights
- GPS device or offline mapping app
- Waterproof outerwear and inner tube spares
- Small first aid kit and a fully charged phone
- Cash for rural honesty boxes, cafés, and unmanned car parks

For your safety and theirs:
Always ride single-file on narrow lanes and watch for sheep on the road. Respect farm gates and never ride across private fields. Stick to designated bridleways if going off-road. Descend slowly — sharp bends and loose gravel are common on steep downhills. Always yield to walkers and use a bell to alert others.

Conclusion:

Cycling in the Yorkshire Dales is both a physical challenge and a soulful reward. With options for every ability and interest, the Dales deliver some of the UK's most scenic, character-rich rides. Whether you're gliding through flower-dappled valleys or grinding up a lonely moorland pass with the wind at your back, every turn of the wheel reveals a deeper connection to this timeless landscape.

8.4 Caving, Climbing & Adventure Skills

The Yorkshire Dales isn't just a place to admire from the surface — it's a living, breathing landscape where adventure runs deep, quite literally. Beneath the rolling hills and limestone crags lies one of the UK's most intricate cave systems, while above ground, natural rock faces offer prime climbing opportunities for beginners and seasoned adventurers alike. Whether you're squeezing through the narrow limestone labyrinth of Gaping Gill, learning to abseil on a sheer crag near Malham, or mastering bushcraft in the wild hills, this region is one of the UK's top spots for outdoor pursuits rooted in challenge, confidence, and exploration.

Description:

Caving in the Yorkshire Dales is a rite of passage for underground explorers. The region's karst limestone has created more than 2,500 known caves, potholes, and passages — many open to guided exploration. Gaping Gill is among the most iconic, a giant 105-meter-deep pothole into which Fell Beck plummets, forming the highest unbroken waterfall in the UK. Each May and August, local clubs erect a winch over the shaft, offering non-cavers the rare opportunity to descend safely to its enormous underground chamber.

For experienced cavers, the Three Counties System — which spans parts of Cumbria, Lancashire, and the Dales — offers miles of passages. Show caves like Ingleborough and White Scar allow families to walk through illuminated underground worlds with stalactites, flowstone, and subterranean rivers — no hard hats required.

Climbers are equally drawn to the Dales' rugged terrain. From bolted sport routes to traditional "trad" climbing and bouldering, the cliffs and edges here cater to various skill levels. Malham Cove is a world-class limestone amphitheatre that attracts elite climbers, while beginners often start with sessions near Twistleton Scar or the limestone outcrops around Kilnsey and Attermire.

Adventure skills courses — including navigation, survival, abseiling, gorge walking, and mountain leadership — are widely available, especially in and around Settle, Ingleton, and Clapham. These activities are ideal for families, school groups, or anyone seeking a structured way to build outdoor confidence in wild environments.

Location:

- **Caving hubs:** Ingleton, Clapham, Horton-in-Ribblesdale
- **Climbing locations:** Malham Cove, Kilnsey Crag, Twistleton Scar, Attermire Scar near Settle
- **Adventure centres:** Settle, Grassington, Austwick, Ingleborough area

Key Features:

- Over 2,500 mapped caves and potholes in the Dales
- Guided cave experiences from beginner to advanced
- Iconic vertical drops like Gaping Gill and Alum Pot
- Trad and sport climbing at world-class crags
- Show caves for family-friendly underground tours
- Skills training: abseiling, bushcraft, navigation, gorge scrambling
- Certified instructors and accredited adventure centres
- Equipment rental and safety gear available locally

Visitor Services:

Outdoor adventure centres like Yorkshire Dales Guides (Stainforth), How Stean Gorge (Nidderdale), and Ingleborough Cave Centre offer structured half-day to multi-day courses in climbing, caving, and outdoor survival. Most centres provide all necessary safety equipment, including helmets, harnesses, wetsuits, and climbing gear. Toilet and changing facilities are standard, and some locations include on-site cafés, picnic spaces, or accommodation. All guides are certified and risk-assessed, and many programs are open to children aged 8 and above with parental consent. Most activities require advance booking, especially during school holidays and summer weekends.

Price:

- Guided caving trips: from $60 to $100 per person (half-day)
- Gaping Gill winch descent (public events only): approx. $20 per person
- Rock climbing experiences: $65–$120 per person (half-day to full-day)
- Bushcraft or survival courses: $60–$150, depending on duration and content
- Equipment rental: often included in guided tours; standalone helmet or harness rental from $15/day
- Family show cave tickets (e.g., Ingleborough Cave): approx. $12 adults, $8 children

Website:

- www.yorkshiredalesguides.co.uk (guided climbing, caving, training)
- www.howstean.co.uk (multi-activity centre including gorge walking)
- www.ingleboroughcave.co.uk (show cave tours and walking routes)
- www.bpc-cave.org.uk/gaping-gill (Gaping Gill winch meets and details)

Pro tip:

Gaping Gill's winch meets only run twice a year and can be weather-dependent. Arrive early — queues build fast, especially during Bank Holidays. Bring waterproofs even in summer — caves stay cold and wet year-round.

Top Adventure Sites to Experience:

Gaping Gill (Clapham):

A dramatic vertical shaft descending into one of the largest natural underground chambers in Britain. Guided access is available only via the winch meets organised by the Bradford Pothole Club (May) and Craven Pothole Club (August). No climbing experience is required — but it's not for the claustrophobic.

Location: Clapham, North Yorkshire (LA2 8EQ)
Price: Around $20 (cash only, subject to cancellation in bad weather)

Website: www.bpc-cave.org.uk/gaping-gill
Opening: May and August winch meets only

Ingleborough Cave & Trow Gill:
Perfect for families and beginner explorers. Follow a scenic woodland walk from Clapham to this well-lit cave full of formations, fossils, and history. Nearby, you can scramble up Trow Gill — a limestone gorge — or hike further to Gaping Gill and Ingleborough.

Location: Clapham (LA2 8EE)
Price: $12 adults, $8 children
Website: www.ingleboroughcave.co.uk
Opening Hours: Daily 10:30 am–4:00 pm (seasonal)

Malham Cove Climbing Area:
A towering curved cliff popular with elite climbers. Most routes are bolted and challenging (sport climbing), though nearby beginner-friendly crags exist. Best tackled with a guide unless you're an experienced climber.

Location: Malham, Skipton (BD23 4DJ)
Note: No gear rentals onsite — book via local guides or bring your own

Twistleton Scar, Ingleton:
Ideal for first-timers. These limestone crags above Ingleton offer single-pitch routes with sweeping views. Local guides often run taster sessions here, combining rock climbing with abseiling and navigation.

Location: Near Ingleton (LA6 3HG)
Book via: www.yorkshiredalesguides.co.uk

How Stean Gorge (Nidderdale):
Located on the eastern edge of the Dales, this action-packed adventure park offers via ferrata, abseiling, caving, gorge walking, and even overnight bunkhouse stays. Perfect for groups, families, and schools.

Location: Lofthouse, Harrogate (HG3 5SF)
Price: Packages from $70 per person
Website: www.howstean.co.uk

Before your trip:

- Book ahead — many experiences fill quickly in peak seasons
- Dress for getting wet: long sleeves, spare shoes, and layered clothing

- Bring gloves, snacks, and a change of clothes for climbing or scrambling
- Confirm age and fitness requirements when booking
- Inform instructors of medical needs or anxiety around confined spaces

Bring the following essentials:

- Quick-drying clothes and waterproof outerwear
- Spare socks and enclosed footwear
- Water bottle and protein snacks
- Small backpack for hands-free exploring
- Head torch for self-guided routes or walking out at dusk
- Pocket first-aid kit and any necessary medications

For your safety and theirs:

Never explore caves or climb alone. Weather can flood caves and make rock faces slippery. Follow guide instructions closely, especially in confined or technical areas. Respect signs marking fragile limestone areas and avoid disturbing bats or nesting birds. Always notify someone of your planned route and expected return time.

Conclusion:

For thrill-seekers and curious explorers, the Yorkshire Dales offer raw, unforgettable adventures both above and below ground. From family-friendly show caves to vertical challenges and survival skills that reconnect you with nature, this region invites you to test your limits while discovering ancient landscapes shaped by water, stone, and time. Whether you're a first-timer or an experienced adventurer, the Dales give you space to explore boldly — and safely — in one of England's most exhilarating natural playgrounds.

Chapter 9: Scenic Routes & Landscape Journeys

9.1 Driving Tours & Rural Roads

The road begins with a hush — not silence, exactly, but that soft, expectant stillness you only find in the Yorkshire Dales. A gate creaks open. A bird flickers past your windscreen. Beyond the hedgerow, sheep graze on hills quilted with wild grasses, stitched together by centuries-old dry-stone walls. Driving here is not about rushing from place to place. It's about moving slowly, letting the landscape unfold around you like a well-worn story, rich with stone, sky, and wind. The lanes are narrow, winding, and often edged with bracken or hawthorn, but they lead to the heart of this place — villages with slate-roofed cottages, valleys with tumbling streams, and wide horizons that stretch your spirit.

Where Every Bend Feels Like a Secret

Each backroad in the Dales feels like it was made for someone in no hurry. You might be hemmed in between stone walls barely wider than your car, or rising steadily into the open moors where sheep roam free. It's not always smooth — there'll be potholes, sheep crossings, and spots with no signal. But that's what keeps it honest. On these roads, you pass fewer cars and more farm gates, see more heather than headlights. It's the kind of drive where you pull over, step out, and just stand quietly because the view is too wide to take in from behind glass.

Buttertubs Pass: High, Windy, and Unforgettable

Description: The Buttertubs Pass, linking Hawes and Thwaite in upper Swaledale, is one of the most dramatic roads in the Dales. It winds tightly along the fellside, climbing high into the hills before opening to expansive views of moorland and valleys. The pass is named after the deep limestone potholes near the summit, where farmers once cooled their butter on market days.

Location: Between Hawes and Thwaite, Upper Swaledale

Key Features: Steep gradients, sharp bends, panoramic views, roadside stops with photo opportunities, occasional livestock on the road

Visitor Services: None along the pass; toilets and cafés available in Hawes and Muker

Price: Free to drive

Contact Address: Hawes National Park Centre, Burtersett Road, Hawes, DL8 3NT

Website: www.yorkshiredales.org.uk

Pro tip: Drive with caution in wet or icy weather — there are no barriers, and fog can roll in quickly over the tops.

The Malham Loop: Limestone, Waterfalls & Quiet Roads

Description: This gentle but scenic circuit wraps through Malham, Malham Tarn, and Settle. You'll drive past grazing sheep, down tree-lined lanes, and across open moor. The route takes in some of the area's most iconic sights — Malham Cove, Janet's Foss, and the sweeping limestone pavement of Malham Tarn.

Location: Circular route from Settle to Malham to Malham Tarn and back

Key Features: Accessible beauty spots, easy lay-bys for walks, views over dry valleys, picnic spots

Visitor Services: Car parks in Malham and Settle, visitor centre in Malham, cafés and loos available

Price: Free to drive; small fees at National Park car parks

Contact Address: Malham National Park Centre, Chapel Gate, Malham, BD23 4DA

Website: www.yorkshiredales.org.uk

Pro tip: Start early in summer — Malham's car parks fill up quickly. Arrive before 9am for quiet trails.

Coverdale to Nidderdale: A Hidden Back Route with Big Surprises

Description: Less travelled but just as beautiful, the road from Carlton in Coverdale to Lofthouse in Nidderdale winds through unspoiled valleys. It's a slow, narrow drive, often single-track, but you're rewarded with endless views, high passes, and the sense that you've slipped into a forgotten part of England.

Location: From Carlton (Wensleydale) to Lofthouse (Nidderdale)

Key Features: Moorland summits, wide skies, isolation, traditional farms, birdlife

Visitor Services: None directly on the route; services available in Pateley Bridge and Middleham

Price: Free to drive

Contact Address: Nidderdale AONB Office, The Old Workhouse, King Street, Pateley Bridge, HG3 5LE

Website: www.nidderdaleaonb.org.uk

Pro tip: Carry snacks and water — you won't pass any shops or cafés for miles. Great for spotting curlews and kestrels.

Dentdale to Garsdale: Quiet Beauty on the Edge of the Dales

Description: This winding route follows the narrow valley of Dentdale, known for its calm, pastoral beauty. The road shadows the River Dee, passing old stone barns and sheep-dotted fields before climbing up into Garsdale's uplands. It's especially peaceful in the early morning when mists still cling to the meadows.

Location: Dent to Garsdale via Cowgill

Key Features: River views, railway viaducts, quiet roads, historic hamlets

Visitor Services: Public toilets in Dent, shops and food in Sedbergh

Price: Free to drive

Contact Address: Sedbergh TIC, 72 Main Street, Sedbergh, LA10 5AD

Website: www.yorkshiredales.org.uk

Pro tip: Pause in Dent village to explore the cobbled streets, small churchyard, and the Heritage Centre — it's full of local stories.

When the Journey Is the Destination

Driving in the Dales isn't about the fastest way from one town to the next — it's about being part of the landscape. Windows down, radio low, breeze carrying the scent of bracken and sheep wool. You'll pass postmen in Land Rovers, farmers at gates, kids walking home from school on roads with no pavements. It's not all postcard-pretty, and it's not always smooth — but it's real. And it makes you slow down, breathe deeper, and remember that travel isn't just where you go. It's how you feel along the way.

9.2 Self-Guided Village-to-Village Walks

There's a quiet kind of magic in walking from one Yorkshire Dales village to another on your own two feet — no need for a guide or group, just a good map, a sturdy pair of boots, and time to follow the old tracks that locals have walked for generations. These self-guided village-to-village routes offer more than just exercise or fresh air; they invite you into the rhythms of daily life, across sheep pastures and limestone lanes, into chapels and cafés where conversations still pause for visitors. You pass through drystone gates, across bubbling brooks, and into hamlets where laundry flaps on stone walls and hikers stop for tea. These aren't just walks — they are cultural connections strung together by history, community, and wild beauty.

From Burnsall to Grassington: Wharfedale's Timeless Heart

Description: This 3-mile walk along the River Wharfe is ideal for beginners or anyone looking for a relaxed introduction to Dales village life. The path hugs the riverbank, leading past meadows, ancient stepping stones, and the graceful stone arches of bridges centuries old. Burnsall's pretty green and riverside church are perfect starting points, and Grassington welcomes walkers with tearooms and artisan shops.

Location: Burnsall to Grassington, Wharfedale

Key Features: Flat riverside walking, birdwatching, stepping stones, wildflowers in spring, benches for rest

Visitor Services: Toilets and cafés at both ends; National Park Centre in Grassington for maps and advice

Price: Free; parking in Burnsall or Grassington (~$6/day)

Contact Address: Grassington National Park Centre, Hebden Road, Grassington, BD23 5LB

Website: www.yorkshiredales.org.uk

Pro tip: Stop at Linton Falls just outside Grassington for a short detour to one of the area's most photogenic spots.

Reeth to Grinton & Marrick Priory: A Swaledale Pilgrimage
 Description: This circular 5-mile walk begins in Reeth and follows quiet footpaths to the medieval village of Grinton and the old monastic site of Marrick Priory. The route weaves together the threads of spiritual heritage and local tradition, crossing the River Swale by ancient bridges and passing through woodland and upland pasture.

Location: Reeth to Grinton and Marrick, Swaledale

Key Features: River crossings, priory ruins, historic churches, field stiles, varied terrain

Visitor Services: Reeth has parking, cafés, a bakery, and a post office; limited facilities in Grinton

Price: Free; optional donation at Grinton Church

Contact Address: Reeth National Park Centre, Hudson House, Reeth, DL11 6SZ

Website: www.swaledale.org

Pro tip: Marrick Priory is now an outdoor centre, but its chapel and monastic history remain. Quiet walkers are welcome to explore respectfully.

Hawes to Hardraw and Simonstone: Waterfalls & Moorland Views
 Description: This 4.5-mile loop walk starts in bustling Hawes, where cheese shops and cobbled lanes create a lively scene, and leads gently uphill to the dramatic Hardraw Force waterfall — the tallest single-drop fall in England. From there, continue through Simonstone and over open moorland, returning to Hawes with views back over Wensleydale.

Location: Hawes to Hardraw to Simonstone and back

Key Features: Waterfalls, moorland paths, panoramic views, sheepfolds, village pubs and cafés

Visitor Services: Parking and food options in Hawes; public toilets at Hardraw

Price: $5 to access Hardraw Force (via The Green Dragon entrance)

Contact Address: Hawes National Park Centre, Burtersett Road, Hawes, DL8 3NT

Website: www.yorkshiredales.org.uk

Pro tip: Walk clockwise in late afternoon light for golden views over the valley and less foot traffic at the waterfall.

Kettlewell to Starbotton: A Classic Dales Stroll

Description: This well-trodden 2.5-mile path between Kettlewell and Starbotton is a favourite among Dales walkers for its balance of accessibility and charm. You follow a section of the Dales Way across pastures, small bridges, and rolling hills, with the ever-changing light making every hour of the day feel different.

Location: Kettlewell to Starbotton, Wharfedale

Key Features: Meadow paths, Dales Way markers, gentle terrain, local stone barns, wildflowers

Visitor Services: Kettlewell has a village store, toilets, and a car park; Starbotton has a tearoom (seasonal)

Price: Free; parking ~$4/day

Contact Address: Upper Wharfedale National Park Centre, Hebden Road, Grassington, BD23 5LB

Website: www.yorkshiredales.org.uk

Pro tip: Combine this with a return loop on the opposite riverbank for variety — or extend to Buckden for a longer walk.

Malham to Kirkby Malham: A Walk Between Limestone Giants

Description: This 5-mile route explores the heart of Malhamdale, linking the bustling village of Malham with quieter Kirkby Malham. Along the way, you'll skirt Malham Cove, pass under sweeping limestone cliffs, and cross farm tracks used since medieval times. This is classic limestone country, full of fossils underfoot and swallows overhead.

Location: Malham to Kirkby Malham

Key Features: Limestone pavement, barn-lined tracks, heritage farms, quiet meadows, rich geology

Visitor Services: Malham has a visitor centre, parking, cafés, and toilets; Kirkby Malham is quieter with a village church and pub

Price: Free; National Park parking ~$7/day

Contact Address: Malham National Park Centre, Chapel Gate, Malham, BD23 4DA

Website: www.yorkshiredales.org.uk

Pro tip: Carry binoculars — this area is a haven for peregrine falcons and wheatears.

Planning Your Self-Guided Walk
Before setting out, always check the weather forecast, as conditions can change quickly in the Dales. Most village walks are well signposted, but having a reliable OS map (Explorer OL2 and OL30 cover much of the area) or a GPS app with offline maps is recommended. Wear waterproof boots — even on dry days, fields can be muddy. Many stiles are made from stone, and gates may require careful handling — close every one behind you. If walking during lambing season (March to May), be especially mindful around sheep.

Visitor Services: Each village mentioned typically offers parking (paid or free), toilets, food shops or cafés, and accommodation. National Park Centres in Grassington, Hawes, Malham, and Reeth provide updated trail conditions, weather forecasts, and maps.

Pro tip: If you're walking between villages, consider using the DalesBus network to return to your starting point. Buses run seasonally and link many key walking routes across the Dales. Timetables are available at www.dalesbus.org.

Conclusion:
Self-guided village-to-village walks in the Yorkshire Dales offer an immersive way to experience the land and its people. Each step takes you deeper into a slower, gentler rhythm, where the sights, sounds, and scents of the countryside unfold without filter or rush. These routes invite curiosity, reflection, and wonder — all at your own pace. Whether you're hiking from Malham to Kirkby Malham under spring blossoms or following the Swale between Reeth and Grinton beneath autumn leaves, the Dales' ancient footpaths will carry you into the heart of northern England's rural soul.

9.3 Trails with Historic & Panoramic Appeal

Where the past walks beside you

In the Yorkshire Dales, some paths do more than guide your feet — they carry the weight of centuries. These trails are old. Worn by shepherds, monks, farmers, and traders. Some cut across moors where Roman legions once marched. Others follow routes medieval pilgrims took on foot, carrying hope in their hearts. And some wind gently past ancient barns and forgotten hamlets, high above quiet valleys where only the wind and curlews speak. The beauty is in the stillness, in the stone beneath your boots, and the way the views open up with each step — grand, wild, and wide as memory itself.

Malham to Malham Cove, Gordale Scar, and Janet's Foss: Three Wonders in One Walk

Description: This 4.5-mile loop near the village of Malham isn't just a walk — it's a journey through limestone history. You'll start with the magical Janet's Foss, a moss-draped waterfall hidden in an ash woodland. Then comes Gordale Scar, a

staggering gorge with cliffs that rise like cathedral walls. Finally, you reach the top of Malham Cove, where centuries of rain have carved a clifftop pavement into natural stone tiles.
Location: Malham village, North Yorkshire, BD23 4DA
Key Features: Janet's Foss waterfall, Gordale Scar gorge, Malham Cove limestone pavement
Visitor Services: Public toilets and parking in Malham; cafés and pubs in the village
Price: Free (parking ~£5/day)
Contact Address: Yorkshire Dales National Park Centre, Malham, BD23 4DA
Website: www.yorkshiredales.org.uk/places/malham

Ribblehead Viaduct & Blea Moor Tunnel Path: Steam, Stone & Open Skies
Description: Near the wild heart of the Dales lies a trail that brushes up against both railway history and natural grandeur. Start at Ribblehead Viaduct — a sweeping arc of 24 stone arches, built by hand in the 1870s. The trail winds toward Blea Moor Tunnel, where Victorian navvies once blasted through rock. Along the way, the moorland stretches wide, golden with grasses, and always under a restless sky.
Location: Ribblehead, North Yorkshire, LA6 3AS
Key Features: Ribblehead Viaduct, Blea Moor Tunnel, views of Whernside
Visitor Services: Free roadside parking, info signs, nearby Station Inn
Price: Free
Contact Address: Yorkshire Dales National Park Authority, Yoredale, Bainbridge, DL8 3EL
Website: www.yorkshiredales.org.uk

Reeth to Fremington Edge: High Paths Above Time
Description: This loop from the village green in Reeth rises steeply onto Fremington Edge, a broad, open ridge that looks down over Swaledale like a quiet guardian. The views go on forever — stone barns, winding rivers, tiny villages tucked in folds of green. Along the way, you pass old lead mine shafts and hushes, scars from a time when this land echoed with picks and the shout of miners.
Location: Reeth, Swaledale, DL11 6SN
Key Features: Fremington Edge ridge walk, panoramic views, lead mining remnants
Visitor Services: Parking, village shops, bakery, museum, tearooms in Reeth
Price: Free (parking ~£4/day)
Contact Address: Reeth National Park Centre, Silver Street, DL11 6SP
Website: www.swaledalemuseum.org

Bolton Abbey to Barden Tower: Abbey Stones and Riverside Calm
Description: Starting from the ruins of Bolton Abbey, this gentle riverside path follows the Wharfe north to Barden Tower, a 15th-century hunting lodge built by the powerful Clifford family. You'll pass stepping stones, lush meadows, and quiet wooded

sections where the sound of water and birdsong make it feel like another time.
Location: Bolton Abbey Estate, BD23 6EX
Key Features: Bolton Priory ruins, stepping stones, Barden Tower
Visitor Services: Multiple cafés, gift shops, toilets, and picnic areas on the estate
Price: Free walk (parking from £15/car/day on estate lots)
Contact Address: Bolton Abbey Estate Office, Skipton, BD23 6EX
Website: www.boltonabbey.com

Pro tip: These trails are best enjoyed slowly — don't rush. Take pauses, notice things: the way moss clings to a gatepost, or how the light hits the valley at noon. Bring snacks, wear good boots, and carry a printed map — phone signals can fade fast.

Conclusion

In the Dales, history isn't locked behind glass — it's under your feet, around each bend, written in the names of streams and crags. Walking these historic and panoramic trails isn't about ticking boxes. It's about feeling the deep hush of time, the wide reach of land, and the quiet welcome of a place that asks nothing but that you walk gently and look closely.

9.4 Public Rights of Way & Open Access Land

Freedom to Roam: The Dales as Your Doorstep

The Yorkshire Dales is one of the few places in England where the land truly feels open — and that's not by accident. Thanks to centuries of custom and legislation, walkers have access to over 2,600 miles of public rights of way, as well as hundreds of square miles of open access land under the Countryside and Rights of Way Act 2000. This means that you can not only follow age-old footpaths, bridleways, and byways through fields and fells, but also legally roam over wide areas of moorland, limestone pavement, and high pasture. This ancient landscape invites you to explore at your own pace, on your own terms, with nothing between you and the horizon but time.

What Are Public Rights of Way?

Description: Public rights of way are legally protected paths across private and public land, including footpaths (for walkers only), bridleways (for walkers, cyclists, and horse riders), restricted byways, and byways open to all traffic (BOATs). They are signposted and shown on Ordnance Survey maps, allowing you to plan routes that cross working farms, old packhorse trails, riversides, and upland slopes. These paths have been used for centuries — some trace Roman roads, others medieval trade routes or shepherd tracks.
Location: Across the entire Yorkshire Dales National Park
Key Features: Clearly signed paths, stiles, gates, green lanes, historical usage
Visitor Services: Free access, public footpath signs, online mapping tools via OS

Maps and the National Park website
Price: Free
Contact Address: Yorkshire Dales National Park Authority, Yoredale, Bainbridge, DL8 3EL
Website: www.yorkshiredales.org.uk/rights-of-way

Where You Can Roam Freely: Open Access Land
Description: Open access land gives the public the right to walk across designated areas without staying on a path. In the Dales, this includes dramatic moorlands, high ridges, limestone plateaus, and remote valleys. These wild spaces allow deeper connection with nature — no walls, no gates, just wind and open sky. However, some restrictions apply during lambing season or for land management and conservation. Always check local signs or the Natural England website for up-to-date access rules.
Location: Prominent access areas include Ingleborough, Malham Moor, Grassington Moor, Whernside, Great Shunner Fell, and Buckden Pike
Key Features: Wild walking experiences, solitude, panoramic views, birdlife and heather moors
Visitor Services: Car parks near access zones, online access maps, information boards at trailheads
Price: Free
Contact Address: Yorkshire Dales National Park Authority, Yoredale, Bainbridge, DL8 3EL
Website: www.openaccess.naturalengland.org.uk

Rules of the Path: Know Before You Go
Description: Although rights of way are open to all, walkers are asked to respect working farmland and local customs. Stay on marked routes where required, close gates behind you, and never disturb livestock. Dogs must be kept on a lead near sheep or wildlife nesting grounds, especially in spring. In open access areas, wild camping, fires, and cycling off-path are not permitted. The goal is freedom with respect — so that future generations can walk these same trails in peace.
Location: Applicable across all public rights of way and open access land in the Yorkshire Dales
Key Features: Countryside Code, signposted rules, conservation zones
Visitor Services: Online guides, local ranger posts, printed maps at National Park Centres
Price: Free
Website: www.gov.uk/government/publications/the-countryside-code

Pro tip: Download the OS Maps app before your walk or carry the Explorer OL Series (OL2, OL30, OL19). These maps clearly mark public rights of way and shaded open access areas, helping you craft spontaneous or planned adventures alike.

Landscapes Without Locks
 The Yorkshire Dales is a rare thing in the modern world: a place where movement isn't restricted, where hills aren't fenced off, and where quiet spaces remain uncommercial and free. These public rights of way and access lands are a national treasure, handed down not by chance but by struggle and civic will. They are for everyone — not just the experienced hiker or the wealthy traveler. They are for families, for pilgrims, for poets, for those who walk slowly and those who climb quickly. When you walk here, you walk in freedom, and you walk in the footsteps of countless others who have gone before.

Chapter 10: Travel Resources & Support

10.1 Official Websites & Information Hubs

Start Here First: The Park's Digital Front Door

Before setting foot on the moors or into a centuries-old market town, the most empowering move you can make is to bookmark the Yorkshire Dales National Park's official digital platforms. These online hubs offer real-time updates, trail maps, accessibility details, seasonal alerts, wildlife sightings, and essential safety guidance — all from the stewards who know the land best. Whether you're looking for walking routes, weather advisories, or local events, this is where informed travel begins.

Yorkshire Dales National Park Authority Website

Description: The official park website is the most comprehensive resource for trip planning. It features detailed guides on hiking, wildlife, conservation, visitor guidelines, and accessibility. You'll find downloadable PDF maps, event calendars, safety notices,

and practical tips for each region of the Dales. It also includes real-time closures, countryside code updates, and current walking conditions.
Location: Digital platform, accessible worldwide
Key Features: Interactive trail maps, educational resources, planning guides, walking route finder, seasonal alerts
Visitor Services: Online trip planning tools, downloadable content, email newsletter, accessibility information, ranger contact
Price: Free
Contact Address: Yorkshire Dales National Park Authority, Yoredale, Bainbridge, Leyburn, North Yorkshire DL8 3EL
Website: www.yorkshiredales.org.uk

National Trails – Pennine Way & Dales Way Resources
Description: For visitors tackling long-distance trails such as the Pennine Way or Dales Way, the National Trails website provides everything from official route guides to GPX downloads and accommodation listings. It's updated with trail condition reports, waymarking details, safety tips, and suggested itineraries that break the routes into manageable day walks.
Location: National network of trail-specific websites
Key Features: GPX files, trail itineraries, accommodation suggestions, travel logistics, elevation profiles
Visitor Services: Route planning support, guidebook links, walker feedback, seasonal notes
Price: Free access to digital resources; optional paid guidebooks
Website: www.nationaltrail.co.uk

North Yorkshire County Council – Public Transport & Travel Updates
Description: For up-to-date information on bus timetables, road closures, and rural transport services across the Dales, the NYCC website is essential. It includes downloadable bus maps, seasonal detours, and connections between key towns and villages, with real-time updates on service disruptions. Especially important for car-free travelers or those using DalesBus routes.
Location: North Yorkshire–wide service
Key Features: Transport routes, bus connections, travel updates, rural transit options
Visitor Services: Live updates, PDF timetables, public travel apps, accessible travel info
Price: Free
Website: www.northyorks.gov.uk

DalesBus – Sustainable Travel Within the Park
Description: DalesBus is a locally celebrated network of buses that connect remote villages and trailheads on weekends and bank holidays. It's the go-to resource for

eco-conscious travelers who want to avoid driving. The website offers a seasonal timetable, route maps, walking itineraries, and suggestions for day trips by bus.
Location: Service runs throughout the Yorkshire Dales region
Key Features: Bus access to walking trails, scenic routes, eco-friendly travel
Visitor Services: Route planning, ticket information, accessibility support
Price: Standard regional bus fares; discounts available with travel passes
Website: www.dalesbus.org

Visit North Yorkshire & Local Tourism Boards
Description: Regional tourism websites such as Visit North Yorkshire or individual village portals like Welcome to Settle or Visit Grassington offer insight into local events, cultural attractions, family-friendly destinations, and independent accommodations. These hubs are useful for insider tips on seasonal markets, festivals, craft shops, and historical walking tours.
Location: Region-wide and village-specific
Key Features: Event calendars, town-specific highlights, culinary tips, local stories
Visitor Services: Accommodation listings, cultural maps, business directories
Price: Free access
Websites:

- www.northyorkshire.co.uk
- www.welcometosettle.co.uk
- www.visitgrassington.co.uk

Pro tip: Always check the National Park's "Know Before You Go" section before setting out. Especially in winter or lambing season, paths may be diverted, car parks may be closed, or ground nesting zones may limit access.

Staying Informed Means Traveling Freely
Reliable information isn't just convenient — it's what allows you to explore the Dales with confidence, spontaneity, and respect for the land. These official hubs are the backbone of responsible tourism: practical, up-to-date, and grounded in deep local knowledge. Whether you're planning a weekend ramble or a two-week circuit of every dale, these digital resources make it possible to move safely, lightly, and meaningfully through one of England's most storied landscapes.

10.2 Travel Apps & Offline Tools

Your Digital Compass in the Dales

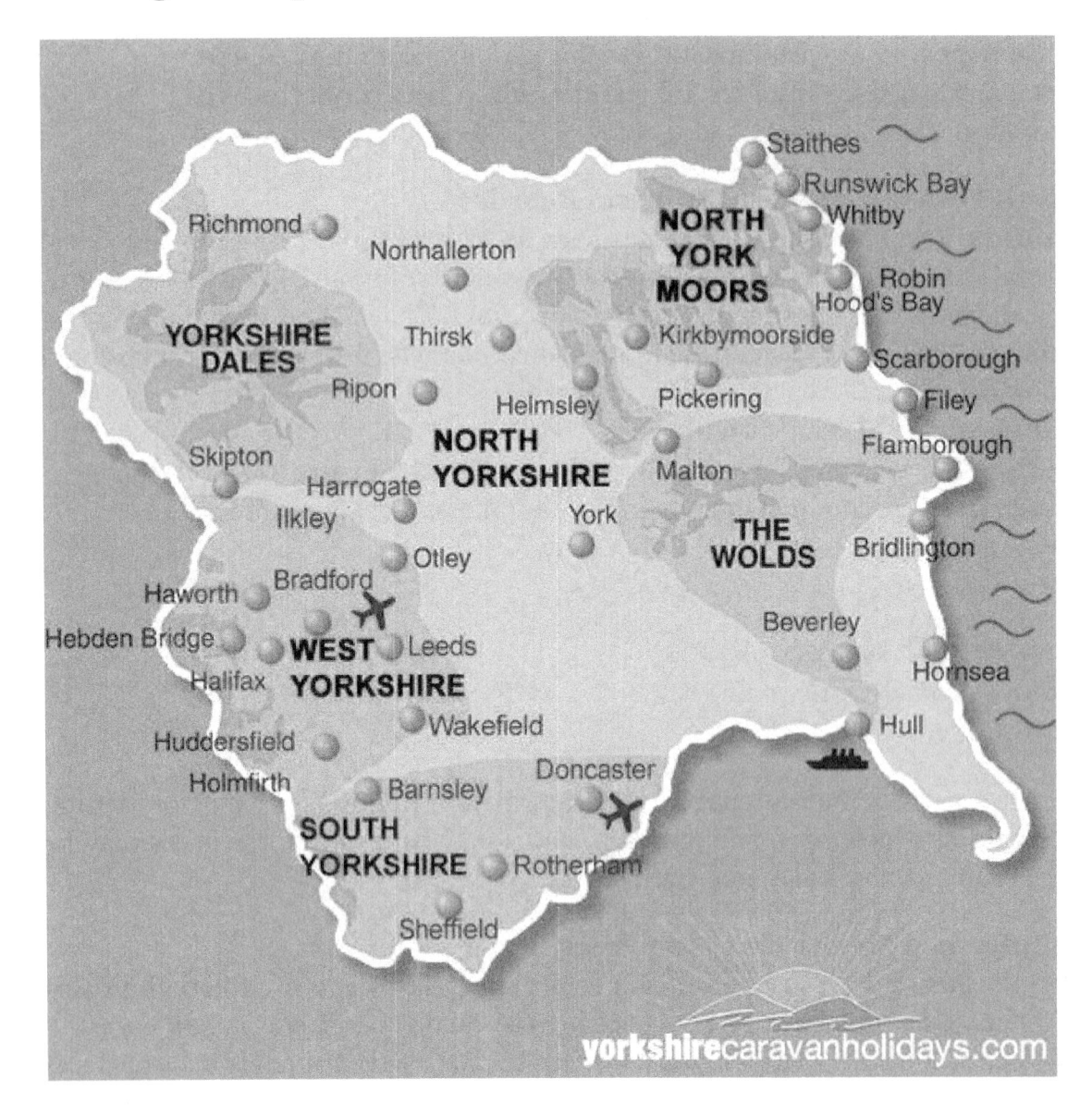

While the Yorkshire Dales offers a glorious escape from modern distractions, digital tools can still serve as quiet allies in navigating its valleys, fells, and footpaths. From downloadable maps to trail trackers and wildlife identifiers, the best travel apps are those that work offline, require little signal, and are tailored to walkers, cyclists, and nature lovers. These tools don't detract from the wilderness — they enhance your ability to move through it with clarity and confidence.

OS Maps by Ordnance Survey
  Description: This is the definitive mapping app for exploring the Yorkshire Dales. OS

Maps offers detailed, topographical maps that can be downloaded for offline use. You can plan, follow, or record your own routes, and the app shows public rights of way, elevation changes, and national trail markers. It's ideal for both seasoned hikers and those unfamiliar with the terrain.
Location: Nationwide coverage with tailored content for the Yorkshire Dales
Key Features: 1:25,000 Explorer and 1:50,000 Landranger map overlays, GPS route tracking, offline mode, elevation data
Visitor Services: Route planning, trail downloads, walking challenges, user-shared routes
Price: Free basic access; full mapping with subscription (~$5.99/month or $32/year)
Website: www.ordnancesurvey.co.uk

AllTrails
Description: Popular among international travelers, AllTrails includes user-reviewed walking, hiking, and cycling routes across the Dales. With GPS tracking, difficulty ratings, and offline trail access for premium users, it's especially helpful for discovering lesser-known circular walks and family-friendly routes.
Location: Global, with strong UK coverage
Key Features: Route finder, trail reviews, waypoints, GPS tracking, offline maps (premium)
Visitor Services: Walking filters (by difficulty, length, activity), weather updates, safety warnings
Price: Free version available; AllTrails+ from ~$35.99/year for offline access
Website: www.alltrails.com

Komoot
Description: Designed for walkers and cyclists, Komoot provides intuitive route planning with downloadable offline maps and voice navigation. You can customize walks by terrain, elevation, and ability, and it integrates well with smartwatches. Especially good for long-distance or multiday routes such as the Dales Way or Pennine Way.
Location: Global coverage with regional optimization for the Dales
Key Features: Turn-by-turn voice navigation, offline mapping, trail difficulty profiles
Visitor Services: Personalized routes, elevation stats, topographic visuals
Price: One region (e.g., Yorkshire) free; full UK region bundle ~$30 one-time
Website: www.komoot.com

Star Walk 2 / Sky Guide
Description: Perfect for night walks or campsite evenings, these apps transform your phone into a star chart. Simply point your device toward the sky to identify constellations, planets, satellites, and meteor showers — especially vivid under the dark skies of Swaledale or Malham.

Location: Works anywhere, no signal required for sky mapping
Key Features: Real-time star maps, celestial calendar, night mode
Visitor Services: Astronomical event alerts, stargazing tools, night sky guides
Price: Free basic version; premium features from ~$2.99–$9.99
Websites: www.starwalk.space or www.skyguideapp.com

What3Words

Description: For safety and coordination in remote areas, What3Words divides the world into 3m x 3m squares and assigns each one a unique three-word identifier. Used by UK emergency services, it's ideal for pinpointing exact trail junctions, campsites, or parking areas in the Dales — especially when reception is weak.
Location: Global grid system
Key Features: Exact GPS location without coordinates, even offline
Visitor Services: Emergency location sharing, trail meeting point marking
Price: Free
Website: www.what3words.com

Merlin Bird ID by Cornell Lab

Description: If you're walking through the bird-rich wetlands of Ingleborough or pausing by the riverbanks of Wharfedale, Merlin Bird ID helps you identify bird calls or feathered sightings. It works offline once bird packs are downloaded.
Location: Global bird recognition, with UK-specific data packs
Key Features: Sound ID, photo ID, species profiles
Visitor Services: Bird library, habitat notes, conservation info
Price: Free
Website: www.merlin.allaboutbirds.org

Offline First: Tools That Work Without Signal

While the Dales have pockets of strong coverage, many valleys and upland routes fall into signal dead zones. Prior to your trip, download maps, trail guides, and relevant data packs to ensure uninterrupted access. Bring a portable charger, and if you're relying on GPS, always have a printed OS map as a backup.

Pro tip: Combine OS Maps for route detail with What3Words for safety and Komoot for voice navigation. This triple setup creates a nearly foolproof digital toolkit for Dales walking.

Travel Smart, Roam Free

With the right offline apps and tools, the Yorkshire Dales open up in new and meaningful ways. Whether you're tracing a Roman road or birding by a waterfall, these digital aids keep you informed and prepared without tethering you to a screen. Used thoughtfully, they become quiet companions — enhancing your journey while keeping your attention where it belongs: on the land, the sky, and the silence between.

10.3 Emergency Services & Park Alerts

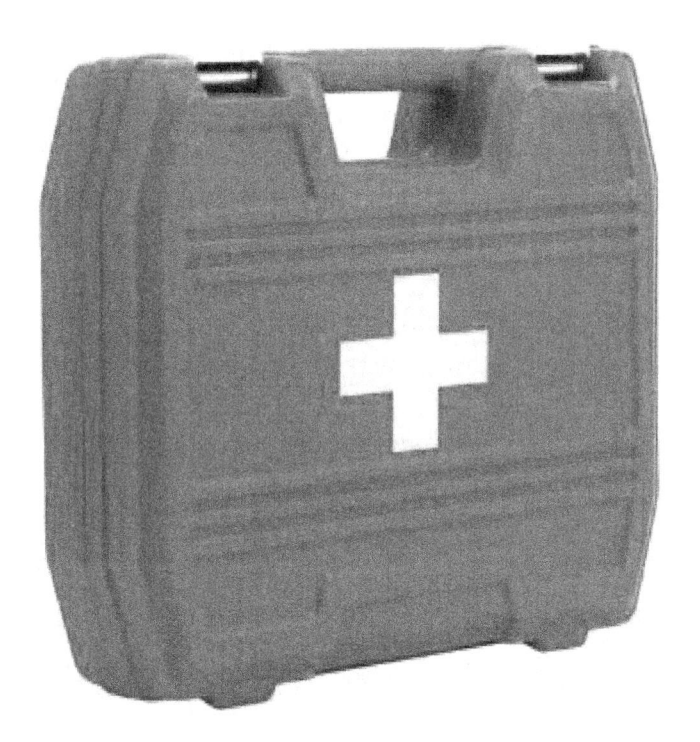

Your Lifeline in the Dales: Staying Informed and Safe

In the expansive, remote, and often rugged terrain of the Yorkshire Dales, being prepared for the unexpected is not optional — it's essential. Whether you're tackling high moorland trails, navigating limestone crags, or exploring hidden valleys, having access to up-to-date emergency information and knowing how to respond to hazards can make all the difference. This section equips you with crucial resources for emergency support, incident response, and real-time park alerts that are tailored to rural, outdoor settings.

Yorkshire Dales National Park Authority (YDNPA) Alerts

Description: The official park website posts real-time alerts concerning trail closures, flooding, landslides, fire risks, and conservation-related restrictions. Particularly during

lambing season, bird nesting periods, or following severe weather, certain rights of way may be temporarily closed or rerouted. Check the alerts before and during your trip, especially if you're hiking, cycling, or wild camping.
Location: National Park–wide coverage
Key Features: Trail and road closures, environmental alerts, safety notices, seasonal access updates
Visitor Services: Interactive maps, downloadable trail updates, ranger notices
Price: Free
Website: www.yorkshiredales.org.uk/category/closures

Mountain Rescue Teams (MRTs)
Description: The Yorkshire Dales is served by volunteer-staffed Mountain Rescue Teams, including Swaledale MRT, Upper Wharfedale Fell Rescue Association, and Cave Rescue Organisation (based in Clapham). These highly trained units respond to emergencies including lost hikers, climbing injuries, falls, or cave incidents. Calling 999 and requesting "Police, then Mountain Rescue" connects you directly to their services.
Location: Region-wide, with coverage across remote walking and climbing areas
Key Features: Emergency wilderness search and rescue, swiftwater rescue, stretcher evacuation
Visitor Services: 24/7 emergency coverage; non-commercial, donation-funded
Price: Free (entirely volunteer-run; donations encouraged)
Contact Address: Swaledale MRT, Catterick Garrison; UWFRA, Grassington; CRO, Clapham, North Yorkshire
Website: www.mountain.rescue.org.uk

NHS 111 & Local Medical Support
Description: NHS 111 provides non-emergency medical advice and help 24/7 via phone or online chat. For urgent, but not life-threatening, issues such as heatstroke, allergic reactions, or injury, they can direct you to the nearest clinic, walk-in centre, or pharmacy in the Dales region.
Location: National coverage
Key Features: Symptom checker, emergency triage, pharmacy locator
Visitor Services: English-language support with translation tools available online
Price: Free
Phone: 111
Website: www.111.nhs.uk

Local Police & Emergency Coordination
Description: North Yorkshire Police provide coverage across the park, responding to incidents ranging from traffic accidents to missing persons. The 999 emergency line should be used for life-threatening or time-sensitive situations. The 101 non-emergency number handles reports such as lost property, livestock incidents, or antisocial behavior.

Location: Park-wide, with main stations in Skipton, Northallerton, and Richmond
Key Features: Patrol coordination, lost person reports, livestock danger calls, suspicious activity response
Visitor Services: Assistance at events, search participation, safety education
Price: Free
Phone: Emergency – 999 | Non-Emergency – 101
Website: www.northyorkshire.police.uk

Met Office Weather Alerts
Description: The UK's national weather service provides detailed, localized forecasts and severe weather warnings that are vital when planning hikes or outdoor activities. Wind warnings, snow, or sudden storms can change trail safety dramatically. Subscribe to email or app alerts for areas such as Ingleborough, Wensleydale, or the Pennine escarpments.
Location: Nationwide, customizable by Dales postcodes
Key Features: Weather warnings, wind speed maps, visibility forecasts, UV and rainfall charts
Visitor Services: Interactive radar, email/text alerts, downloadable weather apps
Price: Free
Website: www.metoffice.gov.uk

Fires, Flooding & Livestock Hazards
Wildfires are an increasing risk in late spring and summer, particularly after dry spells. The park authority may impose temporary bans on barbecues or campfires during high-risk periods. In winter, flooding can quickly make footbridges and river fords impassable. Always check for high river alerts (e.g., on the River Wharfe or Ure). Loose livestock on trails is another real hazard, especially near steep drops or in calving and lambing months (March–May). Keep dogs leashed, give cows wide space, and always close gates securely.

National Park Ranger Service
Description: Park rangers provide mobile safety patrols, trail maintenance, and visitor guidance. If you encounter hazards or become disoriented, they are often your closest source of face-to-face help. Rangers also issue alerts about trail damage, storm debris, or closures.
Location: On patrol across main trailheads and park car parks
Key Features: Trail assistance, safety advice, minor first aid, route confirmation
Visitor Services: Public safety coordination, leaflet distribution, lost item assistance
Price: Free
Website: www.yorkshiredales.org.uk/about/the-authority/our-staff/rangers

Emergency Numbers To Save
Emergency (Police, Fire, Ambulance, Mountain Rescue): 999
Non-Emergency Police: 101
Medical Advice (24/7): 111
Cave Rescue Organisation (Non-Emergency): +44 (0)1729 830455
National Park HQ (Bainbridge): +44 (0)1969 652300
Met Office Weather Service: www.metoffice.gov.uk
Yorkshire Dales Closures & Alerts: www.yorkshiredales.org.uk/category/closures

Pro tip: Mobile reception in the Dales is highly variable. If you're venturing into remote areas like Dentdale, Langstrothdale, or the high moors, download offline maps and write down local emergency numbers in advance. Consider carrying a personal emergency beacon or GPS communicator for multi-day hikes.

Always Prepared, Never Panicked

The Yorkshire Dales is a safe and welcoming destination, but like any wild and open landscape, it demands a mindful approach to personal safety. By knowing where to look for alerts, whom to call in an emergency, and how to anticipate local hazards, you not only protect yourself — you preserve the peacefulness of the place for others, too.

10.4 Weather Forecasting & Local Radio

Understanding the weather is fundamental to safe and enjoyable travel in the Yorkshire Dales. The region's climate is famously unpredictable, and a day that starts with golden light can shift into dense fog or heavy rain within hours — particularly on the high falls and moorlands. Whether you're heading out for a circular walk, cycling along a scenic byway, or driving through a narrow dale, having access to accurate and timely weather forecasts can shape your day and keep you safe. Equally, local radio stations provide not just weather updates but vital traffic information, emergency alerts, and even details about closures, events, and visitor advisories. In areas where mobile reception may falter, they become a lifeline for real-time, location-specific information.

Description:

Weather forecasting in the Dales is a blend of traditional observation and advanced meteorology. The Met Office offers detailed, hour-by-hour updates for individual locations like Settle, Hawes, Reeth, and Malham, including wind speeds, rainfall predictions, UV index, and fog risk. For those trekking at altitude — such as the Pennine Way or Ingleborough summit — mountain-specific forecasts are available through the Met Office's Mountain Weather Service and MWIS (Mountain Weather Information Service). Meanwhile, local radio stations such as BBC Radio York, Dales Radio, and Stray FM provide regional weather news, school closure updates, and road condition reports, making them a critical travel tool, especially when offline. Most radios work reliably across even remote corners of the Dales.

Location:
Forecast services are accessible online and through mobile apps nationwide, while FM/AM radio stations broadcast throughout North Yorkshire and the Yorkshire Dales National Park.

Key Features:

- Hour-by-hour and 7-day forecasts tailored to specific valleys, villages, or peaks
- Mountain weather forecasts highlighting wind chill, cloud cover, summit conditions, and freezing levels
- Weather warnings including amber alerts for storms, floods, ice, and snow
- Local radio bulletins on weather, road closures, livestock incidents, and community events
- Offline reliability for radio even in mobile signal dead zones
- Real-time road condition updates during winter or post-storm travel

Visitor Services:

- Met Office and MWIS apps with customizable notifications
- BBC Sounds app for streaming regional radio broadcasts
- Pocket-sized hand-crank or battery radios available at most outdoor gear shops in places like Grassington, Richmond, and Settle
- Tourist centres often post printed daily forecasts, especially during walking festivals or guided hike events
- Public libraries and cafés in towns like Hawes, Skipton, and Leyburn may provide Wi-Fi for weather checks

Price:
All weather forecast services and radio broadcasts are free to the public.

Contact Address:
Met Office, FitzRoy Road, Exeter, Devon, EX1 3PB
MWIS, Scottish Meteorological Centre, Aviemore PH22 1QH
BBC Radio York: Bootham Towers, Bootham Park, York YO30 7BZ
Dales Radio: Community Broadcast Centre, Sedbergh, Cumbria LA10 5DW

Website:
Met Office: www.metoffice.gov.uk
Mountain Weather Information Service: www.mwis.org.uk

BBC Radio York: www.bbc.co.uk/radioyork
Dales Radio: www.dalesradio.co

Pro tip:
For hikers, check both valley-level and summit forecasts. A clear morning in Kettlewell can mask fog and sleet at Buckden Pike. If you're planning a fell walk, pay particular attention to wind speeds above 600m — anything above 30 mph can make exposed ridgelines dangerous.

Before your trip:
Download the Met Office app and MWIS PDFs for offline access. Set alert notifications for locations like Malham, Reeth, and Sedbergh. Pre-set FM stations (Dales Radio 104.9 FM, BBC Radio York 103.7 FM) on your car or travel radio for reliable updates while driving.

For your safety and theirs:
Rapid weather changes are common. Always carry waterproof gear and an extra thermal layer, especially between October and April. Lightning storms can be fast-moving in exposed regions — descend from high ground if thunder is heard.

Bring the following essentials:

- A reliable weather app with offline capability
- A lightweight radio or car stereo preset with local stations
- Laminated OS maps (paper maps don't run out of battery)
- Spare batteries or a hand-powered charger
- A written list of emergency contacts in case mobile service fails

Conclusion:
Weather forecasting and local radio in the Yorkshire Dales go far beyond basic planning tools — they are part of the lifeline that links you to your surroundings, especially in wild or weather-sensitive zones. The moody skies and dramatic light of the Dales are part of what makes this landscape so poetic and alive, but they also demand respect. With the right information from trusted sources, you'll stay prepared, flexible, and able to adapt your plans without worry. Whether you're a day hiker or a long-distance walker, these tools ensure your journey remains safe, memorable, and grounded in the real rhythms of the Dales.

10.5 Sustainable Travel Tips & Responsible Access

Sustainable travel in the Yorkshire Dales isn't just a trend — it's a commitment to preserving the delicate landscapes, cultural heritage, and rural livelihoods that make the region so extraordinary. From limestone pavements and upland hay meadows to dry-stone walls and sheep-dotted pastures, the Dales are a living, breathing environment shaped by centuries of careful stewardship. As visitor numbers grow, especially in popular spots like Malham Cove, Aysgarth Falls, and Bolton Abbey, the responsibility to minimize environmental impact, support local communities, and protect access routes lies with every traveler. Practicing responsible travel ensures the Dales remain unspoiled for generations to come.

Description:

Sustainable travel in the Dales means making choices that reduce your footprint while enriching your experience. This includes using public transport where possible, supporting small family-run businesses, staying on designated paths to protect fragile ecosystems, and adhering to the Countryside Code. It's about understanding the seasonality of farming and not disturbing livestock or nesting birds, picking up all litter (even biodegradable waste), and refraining from lighting open fires. Travelers can make a difference by choosing accommodations that practice eco-initiatives, avoiding single-use plastics, and walking or cycling between villages rather than driving. Local communities appreciate thoughtful visitors who respect quiet hours, use resources conservatively, and contribute economically without overwhelming services.

Location:

These principles apply throughout the Yorkshire Dales National Park, especially in sensitive ecological areas such as the limestone pavements around Ingleborough, the peatlands above Swaledale, and moorland habitats surrounding Grassington and Buckden. They also apply in cultural zones such as village centres, historic churches, and bustling weekend markets.

Key Features:

- Clear adherence to the Countryside Code and Leave No Trace ethics
- Use of public transport, car-sharing, and cycling to reduce emissions
- Avoiding over-visited trails during peak periods and exploring lesser-known routes
- Respecting livestock, nesting areas, and seasonal farm operations
- Supporting local producers, green-certified accommodations, and ethical tour providers
- Reducing waste through reusables, eco-friendly packaging, and proper disposal
- Encouraging slower travel to reduce strain on infrastructure and foster meaningful engagement

Visitor Services:

- National Park Centres provide maps of low-impact walking and cycling routes
- The DalesBus network connects remote valleys and trailheads, reducing need for car use
- Eco-lodgings and sustainable B&Bs are listed on park-affiliated platforms
- Guided walks with park rangers or volunteer-led interpretation events educate on access and conservation
- Community shops and co-ops often sell locally grown produce and crafts with minimal packaging
- Refill stations for water bottles are located in many villages, cafés, and visitor centres

Price:
Sustainable practices typically cost nothing extra and can even save money (e.g., bus travel vs parking fees, reusable bottle vs buying drinks). Guided educational programs are often free or donation-based.

Contact Address:
Yorkshire Dales National Park Authority, Yoredale, Bainbridge, Leyburn DL8 3EL
DalesBus (transport network): Friends of the Dales, Canal Wharf, Skipton BD23 1RT
Refill Yorkshire Dales (clean water stations): info@refill.org.uk

Website:
Yorkshire Dales National Park: www.yorkshiredales.org.uk
DalesBus: www.dalesbus.org
Refill Stations: www.refill.org.uk

Pro tip:
Skip peak times at hotspots like Malham or Aysgarth by visiting early morning or late afternoon. Not only will you reduce congestion, but you'll also enjoy a more peaceful, photogenic experience with better light and fewer distractions.

Before your trip:
Familiarize yourself with the Countryside Code and current trail conditions. Download local walking maps and the DalesBus schedule. Pack reusable bags, containers, and bottles to cut down on litter and plastic use. Consider offsetting your travel emissions if arriving by car.

For your safety and theirs:
Stay on marked trails to prevent damage to rare mosses, lichens, and ground-nesting birds. Keep dogs on short leads, especially during lambing or nesting seasons (March–July). Don't block gates or access lanes, and avoid playing loud music in natural areas.

Bring the following essentials:

- A reusable water bottle and utensils
- A small bag for litter collection
- Maps or an app for off-the-beaten-path trails
- Sturdy walking shoes that won't damage soft peatland surfaces
- A good understanding of the local area and customs to interact respectfully

Conclusion:

Traveling sustainably in the Yorkshire Dales is not about limiting your experience — it's about deepening it. When you move through the landscape with care, awareness, and respect, the rewards are immense: more genuine encounters, richer stories, quieter moments in nature, and the satisfaction of knowing you're contributing to a long-standing legacy of balance between people and place. Whether you're walking a centuries-old drovers' path or stopping for a slice of local Wensleydale cheese, your mindful choices ensure that these dales, villages, and valleys thrive well into the future.

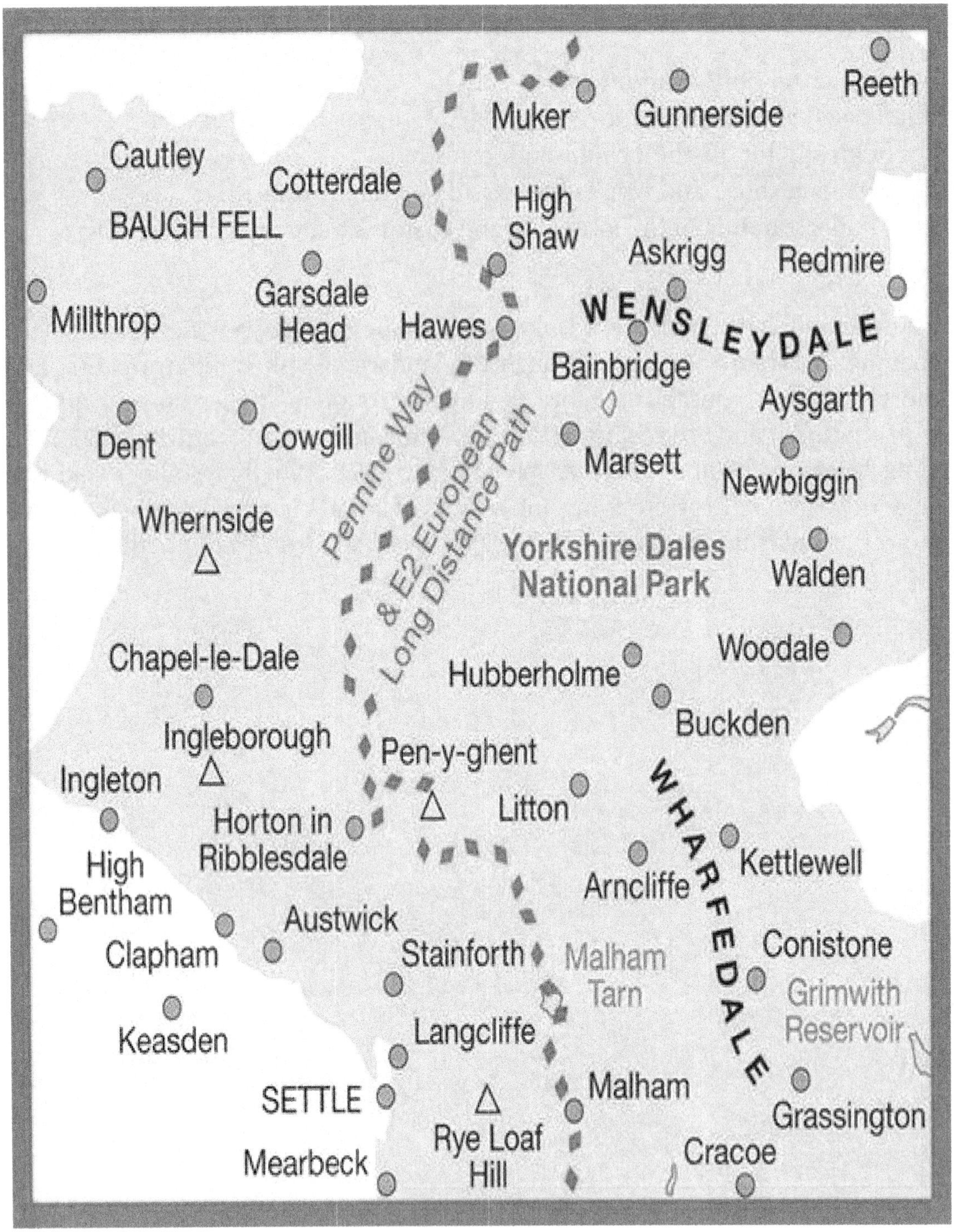
Reeth
Muker
Gunnerside
Cautley
Cotterdale
High Shaw
BAUGH FELL
Askrigg
Redmire
Millthrop
Garsdale Head
Hawes
WENSLEYDALE
Bainbridge
Aysgarth
Pennine Way & E2 European Long Distance Path
Dent
Cowgill
Marsett
Newbiggin
Whernside
Yorkshire Dales National Park
Walden
Chapel-le-Dale
Woodale
Hubberholme
Buckden
Ingleborough
Pen-y-ghent
Ingleton
Litton
WHARFEDALE
Horton in Ribblesdale
Kettlewell
High Bentham
Arncliffe
Austwick
Conistone
Clapham
Stainforth
Malham Tarn
Grimwith Reservoir
Keasden
Langcliffe
SETTLE
Malham
Grassington
Rye Loaf Hill
Cracoe
Mearbeck

Printed in Dunstable, United Kingdom